From
MORMON
to
MYSTIC

*Journey Through Religious Ideology
into Awakened Liberation*

ERIN JENSEN

BALBOA
PRESS

A DIVISION OF HAY HOUSE

Balboa Press books may be ordered through booksellers or by contacting:

Balboa Press
A Division of Hay House
1663 Liberty Drive
Bloomington, IN 47403
www.balboapress.com
1 (877) 407-4847

Because of the dynamic nature of the Internet, any web addresses or
links contained in this book may have changed since publication and
may no longer be valid. The views expressed in this work are solely those
of the author and do not necessarily reflect the views of the publisher,
and the publisher hereby disclaims any responsibility for them.

The author of this book does not dispense medical advice or prescribe the use
of any technique as a form of treatment for physical, emotional, or medical
problems without the advice of a physician, either directly or indirectly. The
intent of the author is only to offer information of a general nature to help you
in your quest for emotional and spiritual well-being. In the event you use any
of the information in this book for yourself, which is your constitutional right,
the author and the publisher assume no responsibility for your actions.

Any people depicted in stock imagery provided by Thinkstock are models,
and such images are being used for illustrative purposes only.
Certain stock imagery © Thinkstock.

Printed in the United States of America.

ISBN: 978-1-4525-2378-1 (sc)
ISBN: 978-1-4525-2380-4 (hc)
ISBN: 978-1-4525-2379-8 (e)

Library of Congress Control Number: 2014918326

Balboa Press rev. date: 11/24/2014

To my husband, my forever huckleberry friend
and
To my mother who embodies the cumulated courage
of all our pioneer ancestors every day of her life

Contents

Stage Five: Conjunctive Faith

Stage Six: Universalizing Faith

ACKNOWLEDGEMENTS

I am indebted to my pioneer ancestors for having the fortitude to trudge through seemingly unbeatable obstacles with unwavering faith. Your determination has passed through the generations onto me.

Thanks to my mother and father. I give my gratitude for your undying love and noble teachings that have deeply enriched all aspects of my life. I was truly born of "goodly parents." And Daddy, you may be gone from this sphere, but your encouraging presence is with me every day.

I am eternally blessed to have been the mother of two sons who have honored me in more ways than I can count. You have imparted many invaluable life lessons onto me, both as children and adults. You are more precious to me than life itself. It is my prayer that you both know how dearly I love you.

For their loving support and for allowing me to claim them as my daughters, I thank both my daughters-in-law. Your gentle presence in our family has enhanced it immeasurably.

I want to acknowledge my seven grandchildren who emblazon the hope of tomorrow into the fabric of our family.

To all my fellow life passengers, especially my brother and sisters, I cannot even begin to thank you for your presence in my life. So gracefully you've touched my heart that mere words are too base to give the thanks you deserve.

A special word of humble gratitude to my mentor and teacher, the late Debbie Ford. I am honored to have known you and to have gone with you on several holy journeys to other lands and into the depths of the heart. It was no mistake that you became an irreplaceable part of my life a mere three years ago. Your wisdom and love pointed me in the direction of my own Light. I am "now ready to dance, to perform miracles, and to fly."

Finally, boundless gratitude I give to my husband, Cliff, for sustaining me through most of my life's passages. You've been my rock when I had nowhere else to turn. *From Mormon to Mystic* could not have been written without your loving encouragement. How fortunate I am to have you walk beside me in this lifetime. My love for you knows no limit. Thank-you!

INTRODUCTION

> . . .The caged bird sings with fearful trill
> of the things unknown but longed for still
> and his tune is heard on the distant hill
> for the caged bird sings of freedom[1]
>
> -Maya Angelou

Debbie Ford is dead. The best-selling author of *The Dark Side of the Light Chasers* succumbed to cancer, February 17, 2013. Over a month later, I sit next to my husband in a large room located in Balboa Park, San Diego. We are at Debbie's Life Celebration. I wouldn't miss this for anything.

I had known her only briefly during the last eighteen months of her life. She was my mentor and I trained as an Integrative Life Coach through her organization, The Ford Institute. A few months earlier, in October, I traveled with her through Italy, Egypt, Israel, and Greece on what she called The Courage Cruise.

Now, on March 23rd, a Saturday, I find myself sitting in a room filled to capacity with over four-hundred people who are there to remember the life of this phenomenal woman. Debbie, realizing her death was imminent, made plans for this event. One thing she knew she wanted was to have the best gospel choir in San Diego perform at her service—this, in spite of the fact that she was Jewish.

Eddie Baltrip and Fulfillment Gospel Choir, consisting of both men and women of African descent, sing praises with "I

Need You to Survive," "Try Him," and "Celebrate." The large chamber fills with euphoric energy radiating from the hearts and voices of the singers. If I lived in the area, I imagine I would want to visit their Sunday services just to get revitalized by the jubilant vocals.

In rhythm with the music—loud, clear, and full of spirit—I feel my own soul transcend beyond the ceiling. I am not alone in my elation. Some of the attendees are lifted off their seats and driven to the aisles where they dance in revelry. Immediately following the first triune of song, spiritual teacher and author, Marianne Williamson, is ready to address the congregation.

Williamson, who co-authored *The Shadow Effect* with both Debbie Ford and Deepak Chopra, begins her address by acknowledging "the shadow first," and appropriately so. You see, Debbie Ford was known as an expert on the shadow and she often referred to herself as the Queen of Darkness.

The shadow is a Jungian archetype that is part of our unconscious minds. It is comprised of all the qualities and beliefs we have about ourselves that we either deny or repress. Sometimes we do both. We usually develop shadow beliefs about ourselves from childhood experiences and conditions. When we don't appropriately deal with our shadow beliefs in our youth, they generally follow us throughout our lives until we process them. Otherwise, they have a tendency to turn pathological.

Marianne continues, ". . . The fact that gospel music can bring us to our feet in celebration the way it does emerges from the fact that it itself emerged from the condition of slavery. Had there not been slavery, there would not have been gospel music."

She goes on to say that the darker the shadow, the greater the light that emerges from it. As soon as she speaks these words, I have one prevailing thought run through my mind, "Mormonism has its shadows!" It hits me hard—the shadows of Mormonism;

and there are many. I should know. I was born into the Church, a sixth generation Latter Day Saint.

I leave Debbie's life celebration that day with new insight and a curiosity about the shadows of Mormonism that I am determined to explore in depth.

The Collective Shadow

Along the same lines as individual shadows, are collective shadows. These take form when one group projects their unclaimed shadow beliefs onto another group. They are expressed as negative qualities or stereotypes. Slavery is an example of the collective shadow. White Americans projected a plethora of negative qualities onto African Americans including the notion that they, blacks, were inferior and therefore should be subject to slavery.

Once I returned home from San Diego, I pondered the idea of the collective shadow as it related to my childhood faith. There was no doubt in my mind that Mormonism fell into the collective shadow category. The Church harbored disturbing secrets from its past and when those murky secrets surfaced, the brethren in the hierarchy would gloss over them or outright deny them as they revised history to fit the need of the day. But most of all, they would blame others by projecting negative qualities onto someone or something else.

All too often it was the doubting member who was at the receiving end of these projections. But other religions fell prey to Mormon projections too, including the Catholic and Protestant faiths. Eventually, the Mormon hierarchy, bustling to become more mainstream Christian, would pretend these projections never took place. But for those of us old enough, the Baby

Boomers, we knew better. We witnessed, first-hand, the temple film where Satan was portrayed as a Protestant minister. And in the canonized Mormon scriptures, the Catholic Church is called the "church of the devil," the "great and abominable church," and the "whore of all the earth."[2] Mormon apologists whisk out inadequate explanations and clarification. But with historical records, science, and archeological and linguistic evidence providing us with Mormonism's authentic history, damage control is how the apologists spend their time and resources. They have an enormous task in front of them. The Church, founded in 1830, is well within the timeframe of impeccable record keeping.

The idea of the Mormon shadow urged me to continue reflecting on my own experiences in the Church. They certainly could not compare to the horrors of slavery. But Mormonism did have its prisoners. I had been one of them. And Mormonism demanded nothing less than complete obedience to the Law of Consecration, one of the oaths I, and all worthy Mormons, took in the temple, "…you do consecrate yourselves, your time, talents and everything with which the Lord has blessed you, or with which He may bless you, to the Church of Jesus Christ of Latter-day Saints, for the building up of the Kingdom of God on the earth and for the establishment of Zion."[3]

The Church held as ransom beloved family members so that if one were to go astray they would break the bond of the eternal family. I was born in the covenant meaning that my parents had been eternally sealed in the temple and therefore all children born to them would be sealed for the eternities as a family unit, provided each child proved to be worthy at the end of her or his lifetime. Admittedly, this was a strong pull and caused many to pretend belief in a church they no longer supported in their heart of hearts.

I left the Church in the mid-1980's; nevertheless, the ghosts of my Mormon past have haunted me throughout the years and I found myself engulfed by them on a daily basis, especially living in Utah.

A common phrase spoken by believing Mormons in reference to apostates (those who not only leave, but speak openly in opposition to the Church) is, "You can leave the Church, but you can't leave the Church alone." There is some truth to what they say in the same sense that a war veteran can return from battle, but can't leave his experience behind or a Holocaust survivor being liberated from Auschwitz continues to write books and give speeches about her ordeal. We don't ridicule the veteran nor do we chastise the Holocaust survivor because we know they are justified in holding onto the lingering phantoms of unspeakable horrors. Like it or not, the atrocities endured have played a role in the shaping of the individual. The same is true for me with Mormonism.

But how could I compare my plight as a multi-generational Mormon to that of the millions who endured slavery, bondage and extermination? It wasn't until several months later that I could come to terms with the discrepancy.

I saw an interview Oprah Winfrey conducted with Diana Nyad who had recently made a record-breaking swim from Cuba to Florida at the age of sixty-four. It was something Nyad said that spurred me to process and eventually understand that *my* experiences, *my* pain, albeit different and less severe, were valid.

Speaking to Oprah, Nyad recounted the time when, as a teen, she was sexually abused by one of her coaches. She blamed herself in many ways as victims of abuse often do. Years later, Nyad gave a talk at a conference where she told this story of molestation to the audience. Later that evening she attended a dinner when an older woman, reaching across a table, exposed the numbers that were etched on her forearm. Diana said, "You're a survivor," meaning a survivor of the Holocaust. The woman shared her personal story with Diana.

At the age of three, the Gestapo came to get her family. Her father told the soldiers that he would not be taken from his home and that they might as well shoot him. With that, one of the soldiers shot and killed him. The three year old daughter witnessed the murder of her father. Her mother and six year old sibling were immediately taken away. She never saw them again. What happened to the three year old? She was taken as a concubine for the SS Officer—at age THREE! Over the next two and a half years she was his sexual slave, forced to do everything.

Diana knew that her molestation, as bad as it was for her, could not compare in its repulsion to the abuse suffered by the woman standing before her. Diana expressed her shame for sharing her "little story" that night. But then, this woman who had been so grossly violated as a very young child said something to Diana that helped her more than anything else in regards to the sexual abuse. The old woman told her not to ever discount her own story. Because "'everyone has their pain and heartache and it's up to all of us to find our way back to light.'" [4]And that's what this book is about—my path back to the light.

It is not my intention to disturb the faith of those who are satisfied with their religious tradition. This book is for those who have struggled in their relationship with faith. It's for those of us who have left a debilitative religion or other unhealthy belief system, but have not yet found a new home.

I spent a large part of my life searching for a spiritual home only to realize I carried it with me all along. I came to understand that each of us must discover for ourselves our own unique spiritual path. Others can act as mentors and point us to the door, but it is up to us to walk through the door that is meant for only us.

I had been immersed for years in a dysfunctional relationship with the Church. And I knew that I had to resolve my dance with Mormonism if I was ever going to move ahead spiritually. Since turning fifty in 2008, I had no time for five-year detours. When I was thirty-nine, I had been given a reprieve on my life when I survived what should have been a terminal illness.

Watching the years tick by all too quickly, I became more and more restless with unresolved issues. The bottom line was that staying stuck was more torturous to me than risking all that I was or thought I was, in order to delve into the unknown. For this, I needed context, something to ground me on this journey through the wilderness of my soul's psyche, *my* final frontier. Eventually I found that context in the six stages of faith, a concept of James Fowler's, retired Professor of Theology and Human Development at Emory University.[5]

Hero's Journey

I determined I would enter into that pathless territory of a faith that was meant for only me, what mythologist Joseph Campbell called the hero's journey, and do whatever it took to gravitate toward and eventually immerse myself into a transcendent reality—whatever that meant. I had dragons to slay and my own shadows to contend with. What I eventually came to understand was that I had the ability to free myself all along.

When I was finally willing to take complete responsibility for my life, my world began to shift exponentially. I came to understand that the experiences I viewed as major obstacles over the years were the very ones that helped me to form the wings I needed to soar. In other words, all the events I had experienced, especially the difficult ones, served as the fuel that would mobilize my transformation from Mormon to Mystic.

Once I began this sojourn into the deepest fissure of my soul, coincidences began occurring every day, and I mean *every* day. So when I say I accidentally stumbled across a podcast about Fowler's six stages of faith and specifically how they related to Mormonism,[6] I knew instinctively that I must use the stages of faith as a backdrop for my own journey through Mormonism and into a realm that transcends all traditions—the realm of the mystics.

Mystics

What does it mean to be a mystic? For me, it is a perceptible shift, in terms of my sense of being separate, to realizing on a visceral and intuitive level that there is a reality that unifies all of us. This reality is transcendent, meaning it goes beyond any concepts of time, space, and form. Because it is experiential, it cannot be adequately described. But when a person makes that shift, they will instinctively know it. For me, it was that moment when my identity transformed from *me* to *we*. The trajectory of my life altered in an instant and I've never been the same since.

I am reminded of when the Buddha came down off the mountain and was asked if he was a god or a man. The Buddha replied, "I am awake." I literally felt like I had awakened from a dream that I thought was reality. Upon awaking, I became keenly aware that I was not limited and isolated. I was and am part of that primordial essence of all that is and so is *everyone* and *everything* else.

Stage Theories

It is our natural inclination to make sense of the world around us and of ourselves within that world. Stage theories help us to do that. They are artificial constructs that are meant to help us understand human evolution in specific areas of discipline. For example, most of us are familiar with the five stages of grief as described by Elizabeth Kubler-Ross: denial, anger, bargaining, depression and acceptance.

The subject matter and development of stage theories vary greatly depending on the psychologist, philosopher, theologian, or educator, who has, through observation, interviews or some other method, perceived a common thread or pattern among the subjects of their study.

There are stage theories for emotions, intellectual development, morality, faith and a host of other areas. They're put into place to make clear what is mostly abstract in nature. What I love most about stage theories is they add context and clarity to otherwise difficult subjects.

When I taught writing at a local college, I often told my students that in order to make the abstract concrete they needed to use analogies, metaphors and examples with which readers could identify. Using the unique characteristics of each stage is one way of doing this. Some of the more well-known names in stage theory, in addition to Kubler-Ross, are Carol Gilligan, Ken Wilbur, Jean Piaget, Lawrence Kohlberg and James W. Fowler.

James Fowler, a Professor emerita of Theology and Human Development at Emory University in Atlanta, Georgia, is also a minister in the United Methodist Church. [7] His book, *Stages of Faith, The Psychology of Human Development and the Quest for Meaning,* first published in 1981, was the result of hours of interviews with people of all ages and faiths. While Fowler was influenced, in part, by Piaget and Kohlberg's work on cognitive and moral development, his stages focus primarily on faith.

During his interviewing and research process, he noted similarities in faith development, regardless of one's worldview. While he did not focus on a specific religion, I, nevertheless, saw the correlation between the stages outlined in his book and my own spiritual evolution. It helped me make sense of what had seemed convoluted and erratic for many years.

Fowler breaks down faith into six specific stages. Stage 1, Intuitive-Projective, begins during our preschool years. It's when our basic ideas about God begin to develop. Fantasy and reality are intertwined.

Once we reach school-age, we enter into Stage 2, the Mythical-Literal stage. We begin to understand the world around us in a more logical fashion and are prone to view the stories we're taught about our faith tradition quite literally.

With few exceptions, by the time we are teenagers, we enter into the third stage of faith, what Fowler calls the Synthetic-Conventional stage. During Stage 3, we begin to identify with and adopt a specific faith tradition; in my case it was Mormonism. At this stage, people live "inside the box" of their religion and very often don't realize they are there. Authority, in Stage 3, is placed in specific religious leaders and the religion itself. Many people remain in this stage for the duration of their lives.

Those who move on enter the Individuative-Reflective Stage 4. This usually begins in early adulthood, oftentimes when one leaves their childhood home and ventures into the world where they are exposed to new ideas. Stage 4 individuals begin to critically examine their previously held beliefs on their own and often become dissatisfied with the faith of their younger years. Stage 4 can be wrought with difficulties as a person comes to terms with what they really believe. That's why it is common for people in Stage 3 (those who accept their faith tradition at face value) to view those who have moved to Stage 4 as backsliders when in reality they are progressing in terms of their faith journey. Many stay in Stage 4 their entire lives, but there's an incredible payoff for those who transition into the next phase.

One rarely reaches Stage 5, Conjunctive Faith, before mid-life. During this time, a person begins to understand the limitations of logic. They are now able to see and accept the value of life's paradoxes. Sometimes people in this stage will return to the sacred stories of their youth or other tradition, but in a decidedly different fashion. Symbolic and allegorical interpretations are valued and keep the person from getting stuck in a theological mindset that is characteristic of Stage 3 individuals. I view the entering of Stage 5 as the beginning of my mystical life.

The final stage is the rarest of them all. Very few people ever make it to Stage 6, Universalizing Faith. We may have glimpses into this transcendent stage where our focus turns away from ourselves and onto others, but for the most part, we rarely live within it at all times. There are, of course, a few exceptions. As we continue along our paths as mystics and reach this final stage of faith, we begin to fully comprehend the nature of non-duality and unity in all things. Compassion and service become primary even to the point where one's own safety may be of little concern. [8]

Transformation

As I began to trace my spiritual journey alongside Fowler's stages, a profound understanding about my own evolution in faith emerged. At the time I began this passage, I was firmly planted in Stage 4, Individuative-Reflective. I was questioning all my prior beliefs and was struggling with who I was and where I was going.

While I was exploring a vast array of philosophical and spiritual ideas, I had been catering to my intellect, but was woefully neglecting my heart and intuitive sense. I had allowed myself to be consumed by my story of victimhood and the "poor me" emotions that went along with it. I was all too ready to put blame for any troubles I had in life on the Church or some aspect of it.

As I studied the different stages, I found that Stage 4 was the most difficult one for me to navigate through. But as time moved on, I began to experience hope that I could and would wind my way out of the chasm of what seemed like endless blame, ridicule, doubt, and many dark nights of the soul. If I could but face that which seemed unbearable and march through the armies of fear, frustration and disbelief, I could reach a place of emancipation where tranquility, love, and compassion would be my rewards.

I spent months doing shadow work where I forged my own path in search of the Holy Grail that lay hidden within my psyche awaiting the day where I would be ready to lay claim to this seemingly elusive treasure that held the power to liberate my soul. I began to believe that I would come to know peace—a peace "which surpasses all understanding."[9]

I wanted a complete transformation where my life would morph into something unrecognizable to what it had been and it was hope that was going to get me there.

If, like me, you are at a point in your life where you know that who you are is no longer an option and the beliefs you once "knew" were true no longer resonate with you, but you're not sure what that means in terms of your own spirituality and belief in God, if there even is a god, then I invite you to continue to travel with me through the following pages.

It is my desire that my journey will act as one of many potential options as you follow your own path from doubt and uncertainty to an understanding of your own transcendent nature that you, and only you, will determine.

I will show you how I uncovered my darkest shadows and illuminated them so they could be examined and eventually embraced. And through understanding the process of integrating illuminated shadows with the intuitive self that is laden with potential, you may be able realize that you, too, can also transcend into a realm of exquisite understanding and peace.

You will never be alone throughout this journey, even if at times it feels like it. You are always in the company of the most sacred part of yourself that you may not even realize exists—yet. And when you reach that most sacred of places you will come to acutely know that there is an interconnectedness of all beings—a unity. Within this unity, I am waiting. It is as the Sufi poet, Rumi, put it, "Out there beyond notions of wrongdoing and right doing. . . there is a field. I will meet you there."

STAGE ONE

Intuitive-
Projective Faith

CHAPTER 1

Lions And Tigers And Bears, Oh My!

Now I lay me down to sleep, I pray the Lord my soul to keep, If I shall die before I wake, I pray the Lord my soul to take.[10]

-New England Primer

Before I jump into the first stage of faith development, I want to briefly describe the pre-one stage that begins at birth and lasts until age two during language acquisition. This pre-stage is when an infant gets a sense of the world being safe or unsafe. Of course, babies lack the cognitive ability to determine this, but they do know that when they cry someone comes to them—or doesn't.

We've all heard or read about babies who were not nurtured, or spoken to, or who were badly neglected. They became emotionally compromised, and if there was no intervention, they may have encountered difficulties interacting with others throughout their lives. If, however, a baby was nurtured, cuddled and cooed to, then she is more likely to grow into a healthy person who is able to function within society.[11]

By the time a child becomes a toddler, he has entered Stage 1—the Intuitive-Projective stage of faith, which generally lasts until the child enters school.

While in this stage, the child often cannot discern between reality and fantasy. Magical thinking is present. For example, a child may really believe that if she is good and does what she's told, Santa will bring her what she asks for.

While interviewing preschoolers for his research, Fowler asked the children to share "what kinds of things make them feel fearful or afraid." Virtually every answer was "in some variant of lions, tigers, bears and monsters."[12] Even when the children were reminded that they rarely, if ever, saw these things in their daily lives, they responded to the same question asked a second time in the same way. Children may not see these creatures in real life, but they often dream of them. They lack the cognitive skill to distinguish between these dreams (or cartoons) and actuality.

I remember an outing I had with my three-year-old grandson whose parents had just become new Christians. It was the holiday season and my grandson and I were walking through an outdoor Christmas village. There was a nearly life-size nativity ensemble with angels, barn animals, Joseph, Mary, and, of course, the baby Jesus in a manger. I thought his parents might appreciate me drawing my grandson's attention to this scene. I pointed to the baby Jesus and asked, "Sweetheart, do you know who that baby is in the manger? Who is that baby?" My grandson looked puzzled so I added a couple of hints. "See the angels and the shepherds? Do you know who he is?"

My grandson pondered this question a moment and then with an expression of understanding he said, "It's baby Spiderman!"

After I finished snickering, I said, "Do you think it might be baby Jesus?"

"Yeah," he said as he nodded, "It's baby Jesus."

Because he was familiar with the Spiderman fantasy figure, that's the conclusion he initially drew. An older child, having more life experience and mental development may have considered the other features in the scene such as the angels, the livestock and the manger, and drawn a different conclusion.

It is during this first stage that children receive their initial concept of God, either through parents, society, or some other means such as Sunday school. When a child attends church, they are likely to see pictures or statues of religious figures. Mormons hang anglicized pictures of Jesus on the chapel walls. In the church of my childhood, there were pictures throughout the building of Mormon founder, Joseph Smith and the First Presidency that included the current prophet and his two councilors. Photographs of temples, particularly the Salt Lake Temple were there as well. The only picture of God that I remember was a rendition of the official version of the First Vision when fourteen-year-old Joseph Smith entered into the Sacred Grove. [13]

During Stage 1, children can develop a fear, oftentimes a great fear, of death, but without fully understanding what it is. Perhaps they lose a pet or a grandparent. This is where fairytales can prove to be helpful. These types of stories serve to alleviate the anxiety a child has. I can't help but think of Snow White and Sleeping Beauty, who both appeared to be dead. They were saved from eternal slumber, when their prince kissed them tenderly on the lips and brought them back to life. That notion resonates in a child's mind.

Scary circumstances and feelings can be remedied by such stories, thereby lessening the anxiety felt by the child. Bible stories, particularly those with comforting resolutions, also serve the purpose of lessening a child's fears.[14] Admittedly, I have little memory of what was taught to me during this phase other than the story of how Mormonism got its start. But it was enough to give me a sense that we, as Mormons, were in God's favor.

CHAPTER 2

A Peculiar People:
Mormon Origins

I will make a few remarks upon the idea of our being
a peculiar people . . . and if we look upon ourselves
from a proper point of view, we shall readily
admit that in this respect outsiders have given us
an appropriate name; for we are a peculiar people
whom God has chosen to serve and honor him.[15]
> – Orson Hyde, *Journal of Discourses*

In the fertile climate of The Second Great Awakening,
Mormonism, often described as the quintessential American
religion, emerged in upstate New York in the first half of the
nineteenth century. The area where founder Joseph Smith lived
was known as the Burned Over District because it was here
that the fervor of revivals and the formation of new religious
movements took place.

In 1820, fourteen-year-old Joseph Smith, disillusioned by
the many protestant religions vying for members, went into a
nearby grove—known as the Sacred Grove—to pray to know
which church he should join. While he was there, he had a
vision. There were numerous versions of the First Vision. I am
aware of at least seven. The official Church version, written in

1838, claimed that two personages, God the Father and His son Jesus Christ, appeared suspended in air, before Joseph Smith.

God said, "This is My Beloved Son. Hear Him!"[16] Jesus then told Joseph that none of the churches were true, and that he should not join any of them. One would suppose that this event would have changed Joseph's life from that moment on, but he seems to have gone on as usual, treasure hunting with his father and tending to the farm. The story did not continue until Smith was seventeen.

While we have a surfeit of information in historical records and journals that were written by Smith and those who knew him, in many ways, Joseph Smith remains an enigma to this day. We know that he was born in Sharon, Vermont, in 1805, the fourth child born to Joseph Smith, Sr. and Lucy Mack Smith. The family would eventually move to Palmyra, New York where Joseph's visions began. But he was not the first in his family to have visions. Both his father and his grandfather reported having visionary dreams.

Joseph's father was a Universalist, while his mother, Lucy Mack Smith, leaned toward Presbyterian teachings. So, theological divisions were evident, not only in the geographical area in which the Smiths lived, but also within the Smith household. This could explain why, in later years, Joseph claimed that revivals occurring in 1820 precipitated his going to the Grove. Historical records indicate otherwise. Nevertheless, the confusion in his home could have certainly led to his own confusion.

After the First Vision, the story recounted Joseph's numerous meetings with angels, including the Angel Moroni who appeared in Smith's bedroom on September 21, 1823—the Autumnal equinox which is highly relevant. ". . . The angel had appeared on the night of the autumnal equinox, between midnight and dawn–hours auspicious for a magical invocation . . ."[17]

The angel told Joseph of secret ancient records written centuries earlier on golden plates. Joseph was told that the plates were buried deep within the Hill Cumorah, near the Smith home. After several years, Smith claimed that he secured the plates. By that time he had fallen in love with Emma Hale, the daughter of Isaac and Elizabeth Hale. Much to the disappointment of Emma's father, she and Joseph eloped in 1827. It seemed that from that point forth, Mr. Hale resigned himself to having Joseph as a son-in-law.

Once the golden tablets were in Joseph's possession, he commenced the translation process. It was not done in a scholarly fashion, but rather consisted of him placing a seer stone into a large hat. Next he placed his face over the opening of the hat in such a way that it was completely dark within. This seer stone helped Smith translate the plates from what he called reformed Egyptian into English.

The plates were always covered with a cloth. At times, they were not even in the room with him during the translation process. Several scribes, including Martin Harris, Michael Morse, Joseph Knight Sr., Emma Hale Smith (Joseph's wife), and others testified to this method of translation.[18] The end result of this process was *The Book of Mormon*.

Years later, nineteenth century American writer, Mark Twain made a visit to Salt Lake City, Utah. He wrote of his experiences amongst the Mormons. While there he obtained a copy of *The Book of Mormon*. He had this to say about it,

> All men have heard of the Mormon Bible, but few except the "elect" have seen it, or, at least, taken the trouble to read it. I brought away a copy from Salt Lake. The book is a curiosity to me, it is such a pretentious affair, and yet so "slow," so

sleepy; such an insipid mess of inspiration. It is chloroform in print. If Joseph Smith composed this book, the act was a miracle—keeping awake while he did it was, at any rate. . . The book seems to be merely a prosy detail of imaginary history, with the Old Testament for a model; followed by a tedious plagiarism of the New Testament. The author labored to give his words and phrases the quaint, old-fashioned sound and structure of our King James's translation of the Scriptures; and the result is a mongrel . . . Whenever he found his speech growing too modern—which was about every sentence or two—he ladled in a few such Scriptural phrases as "exceeding sore," "and it came to pass," etc., and made things satisfactory again. "And it came to pass" was his pet. If he had left that out, his Bible would have been only a pamphlet.[19]

The Book of Mormon is the story of an Israelite, Lehi. Around 600 BC, he traveled with his family by ship from Jerusalem to America. Lehi's descendants consisted of two tribes, the Nephites and the Laminites. The two tribes warred with one another for centuries. Ultimately, Jesus Christ appeared in America after his crucifixion and resurrection. His arrival, along with his teachings, began a period of two hundred years where there was peace between the two tribes. Eventually, however, the Nephites and the Laminites went back to their earlier conflicts.

One of the Nephites, a prophet named Mormon, wrote the story of his tribe on golden tablets. On the day before the final battle, Mormon handed over his written records to his son Moroni. In the ensuing battle, Mormon was killed at a place called Cumorah. Moroni was the last surviving prophet from the Nephites. He lived another thirty-six years and added to the record before finally sealing it up in 421 AD.[20] And that's where they remained until Joseph Smith, following the visit from the Angel Moroni, went to the Hill Cumorah where he uncovered the hidden plates. After Smith finished the translation process, he said the Angel Moroni carried the golden plates away.

What made this story so very American was that an ordinary farm boy from rural New York witnessed miracles. The god he claimed he saw was the same God of the Old Testament. If these miracles were to be believed, it meant that anybody, even the most base and ordinary of persons could receive revelations and become a prophet just like the prophets of old. This notion fit in nicely with the American dream where a common person could rise to the highest office in the land.

Mormonism was a religion that sprouted from the soil of America and its founder was an ordinary son of a farmer. Add to this the intelligence and charismatic nature of Joseph Smith and it's easy to understand how easily he drew people to him and his Mormon bible. But what really made this new faith stand apart from the others was that there was an actual book, published in 1830, that was concrete and tangible. A man or woman could purchase it, hold it in their hands and read it. For many, seeing *The Book of Mormon* in print added credibility to Joseph's story.

While Smith may have had his followers from the beginning, he also had his critics. Joseph's new religion did not set well with the Methodists, Presbyterians, and other Christian sects. Joseph claimed his religion to be the one true church. He claimed that Christianity fell upon a world-wide apostasy and became corrupt for some eighteen-hundred years. He did, in essence, say that all Christian denominations were not only part of that corruption, but continued to perpetuate it.

Skeptics questioned *The Book of Mormon* and considered it fraudulent as well as blasphemous. Other religious leaders saw Joseph as arrogant when he quite literally attempted to obliterate their nearly two thousand year old belief system. Smith added to their mistrust when he restored the office of prophet (an office that according to many Christian theologies, had died on the cross with Jesus) and declared himself a prophet for a new era. His claims were extraordinarily offensive to many community members.

Eventually, Joseph Smith left town and traveled to Kirtland, Ohio where he hoped to create a theocratic commune—a Zion. He took seventy-five people with him and met up with Sidney Rigdon, a former Baptist minister, who brought along one-hundred of his own congregates. Brigham Young, a new convert, also met up with the Mormons in Kirtland.

In 1831, Joseph Smith began sending missionaries throughout America. Within a few years, the town of Kirtland boasted about three-thousand citizens, mostly Mormon. It was during this time that Smith began calling his followers Latter Day Saints (LDS), because of the belief of the impending second coming of Christ where He would reign for a thousand years before the final judgment. Mormons, like other denominations from The Second Great Awakening, adhered to this millennial belief. This may not have been terribly odd in light of the times, but Smith receiving revelations was.

Revelation was, and is, paramount in Mormonism. As odd as Smith's religion was up to that point, he flew into a flurry of new revelations that made the Mormons and their beliefs even more peculiar than before. Through his revelations, Smith brought forth the roles of the twelve apostles. All worthy males received the priesthood.

Inspired by the Old Testament, Smith would have a temple erected where secret oaths and rituals would be performed—different from those described in the Bible. It was there, in the temple, where the Latter Day Saint could connect to God. In present day temples, the same is believed. The temple experience is considered the pinnacle of spiritual connection to the divine. In Smith's time, folklore began to develop that added to the richness of the temple experience. Members claimed to miraculously hear choirs of angels. They had visions and hallucinations experienced en mass.

When I was in college, I enrolled in an honors folklore course. I became enthralled with the peculiar lore of the Mormons. I heard countless stories of the Three Nephites,[21] angelic relatives assisting their living descendants with their genealogy work, and sightings of spirits by temple goers who acted as proxies to complete the necessary work that the dead would need in order to achieve the highest level of exaltation. It was commonly believed that these souls could not be at peace until they knew the work had been done for them.

Utah is filled with a plethora of folk tales and I never tire of hearing them. The tradition that seemed to start, at least in the Mormon way, in Kirtland, is alive and well in modern times.

While in Kirtland, Ohio, Joseph Smith started a bank and entered into several business ventures. Eventually the ventures failed and the bank went belly-up. When people began losing their money, they also began questioning Smith's veracity as a prophet of God. In addition, there were rumors about Smith's sexual indiscretions. Later, we would learn that he began the practice of plural marriage—polygamy—during his time in Ohio. At the height of his practice, he had thirty-three wives of whom I'm aware, in addition to Emma. Seven were under the age of eighteen and eleven of them were already married to other men who were still living, a practice known as polyandry.[22]

Smith lost favor with many Ohioans as well as some members of his own church. Add to that the financial problems he experienced and possible lawsuits that were pending and it seemed to Joseph that the best thing to do was to get out of town. He ended up in Jackson County, Missouri where the shadow of persecution would be firmly cemented in the psyches of the Mormons.

According to one of Joseph Smith's revelations, Zion was to be found in Missouri. Smith revealed to his followers that the Garden of Eden, where Adam and Eve tread before the original sin, was located in Independence, Missouri. This belief traveled through the decades to me. It was frequently discussed when I was growing up that one day we, the Mormons, would be beckoned back to Missouri to await the Second Coming of Christ.

Joseph's continued revelations caused native Missourians to grow suspicious of him and they tried to make life miserable for the Mormons. There were numerous stories of Mormons being tarred and feathered and forced out of their homes and off their lands. The Church members, it seemed, paid a high price for the supercilious nature of their leader.

Smith, not to be mistaken for a Quaker, formed his own militia. The Mormons would not turn the other cheek. With each strike against them, they fought back. It came to a head with an act so violent that it was difficult, if not impossible, to justify.

In the autumn of 1838, a mob rode into Haun's Mill, a Mormon settlement in Caldwell County, Missouri. The mob surrounded the blacksmith shop where the Mormon men were holed up. Sticking their firearms through openings between the logs, the mob shot at the Saints. In the end, seventeen Mormons were killed that day in what was called the Haun's Mill Massacre. No one was ever arrested for the murders.

To end the violence between the Missourians and the Mormons, Governor Lilburn Boggs took an unprecedented act. "For the first and only time in American history, a state government issued an extermination order. 'The Mormons must be treated like enemies,' it read, 'and must be . . . driven from the state for the public peace.' The Mormons were forced to surrender their land and possessions and to be out of Missouri by spring."[23]

Although there was little doubt that the Mormons experienced persecution, there were varying opinions as to how much of it was brought on by the Mormons themselves. It certainly seemed obvious that their leader was responsible for much of the hardships that the members endured. Regardless of fault, Haun's Mill soundly put the label of "persecuted" in the minds and hearts of the Saints. Historian, Sarah Barringer Gordon said this,

> Mormons have a very complex relationship with their own sense of persecution. . . it brought them exhilaration and conviction that what they are doing was the right thing . . . Persecution both identified them as special and seared into them a pain of what being a peculiar people meant.[24]

The Mormons were on their way again to another place that they might call Zion—Nauvoo, Illinois. It would be the last leg of the journey for Joseph Smith.

The people of Illinois, having heard of the atrocity at Haun's Mill, welcomed the Mormons. Smith purchased property and began creating a new home for the Saints who grew in numbers as converts from Europe and Scandinavia joined them. With hard work, homes and factories were built and by 1844 the population increased to twelve thousand—nearly equal to that of Chicago.

While in Illinois, Joseph again had a surge of new revelations including baptism for the dead. A living person acting as proxy could receive the ordinance of baptism for their deceased loved one, thereby ensuring they would live in the eternities with their family member.

Years earlier, in 1823, Joseph's older brother, Alvin, died unexpectedly. His death devastated the family. Joseph's mother, Lucy, was especially distressed because Alvin died without being baptized. This new revelation fixed all that. Alvin, from the spirit world, could accept the baptism performed for him as if he had done it himself while still alive. Baptism for the dead enabled anyone who lived before the Church was created or who did not accept the Church in their lifetime to now receive the full benefit of being baptized.

Another major revelation, celestial marriage, came forth in the Nauvoo years, ". . . the ancient order of Plural Marriage was again to be practiced by the Church."[25] Although Joseph and other high-ranking Mormon men had already been secretly practicing celestial marriage for some time, it was not officially recorded until 1843.

One could argue that Joseph Smith, in the beginning, knew he was perpetrating a fraud. But it seemed that by his Nauvoo years, he began to believe he was a prophet of God. There were definite signs of delusions of grandeur. In addition to secretly practicing polygamy,

> Joseph Smith launched himself on a path of self-destruction, obsessed with building his military and political power. . . He was elected mayor. He had himself appointed chief justice of the city and

lieutenant general of the Nauvoo Legion. Nauvoo
had become a perfect theocracy and their neighbors
increasingly saw that Mormons' dominance as a
threat.[26]

In 1844, Joseph Smith ran for president of the United States.
He chose as his running mate, Sidney Rigdon. Missionaries
were sent out to campaign for Smith and Rigdon. While Smith
made numerous tactical errors, there was one that cost him
much more than the election. It cost him his life.

William Law, a high-ranking Mormon, left the Church for
various reasons, including Smith's practice of polygamy with
which Law did not agree. Law founded a newspaper, *The Nauvoo
Expositor*. The first and only issue, dated June 7, 1844, revealed
Joseph's practice of plural marriage, among other things. In
part, because of his political aspirations, Smith did not want to
get found out. He ordered the destruction of the press.[27]

Americans, then and now, take First Amendment rights
very seriously. You simply did not compromise freedom of the
press. Joseph Smith learned this the hard way. He was arrested,
charged with treason and incarcerated in the Carthage Jail.
Other arrests were made including John Taylor, who became
the third President of the Mormon Church, and Hyrum Smith,
Joseph's brother.[28]

John Taylor made a statement concerning the events leading
up to the prophet's death. In it he stated that the prisoners
received a visitor, Elder Cyrus H. Wheelock. Before he left,
Elder Wheelock pulled out a pistol—a six-shooter—and offered
it to the prisoners. "Brother Joseph immediately replied, 'Yes,
give it to me. . .'"[29]

Soon after this exchange, a group of men began ascending
the stairs leading to the jail cell. There were shots fired. Joseph's

brother, Hyrum, was killed. Taylor recounted that Joseph, leaning over the body of his dead brother said, "Oh! my poor, dear brother Hyrum!"

Right away, Joseph approached the cell room door and using the gun Wheelock gave him, opened the door slightly and began shooting toward the mob. Taylor testified that Smith shot three men, two died from their wounds.[30]

Joseph Smith dropped his gun and went to the window. From the cell door, two rounds hit him. Now mortally wounded, Smith cried, "Oh Lord, My God," before falling from the second story window to the ground below. Some accounts, including that of John D. Lee, the adopted son of Brigham Young and the only one executed for the 1857 Mountain Meadows Massacre,[31] stated that Joseph, who was a freemason, uttered as his last words the masonic cry of distress, "'OH, LORD, MY GOD, IS THERE NO HELP FOR THE WIDOW'S SON!'"[32] Knowing that many if not most of the mob members were Masons, this was probably Smith's last attempt to save his life.

I've often wonder if the Church would have endured had Smith not been murdered. Upon his death, he became a martyr in the eyes of many. From 1845 to the early 1930's part of the endowment ritual in the Mormon temples included the oath of vengeance where participants vowed to pray to God to avenge the deaths of the prophets Joseph and Hyrum Smith.

Many active Mormons today are not aware of the fact that Smith had a gun and killed two men before being gunned down. While I don't criticize Smith for self-defense (I imagine many of us would do the same thing in his situation), what I find curious is that Smith was lifted to the status of martyr, "like a lamb to the slaughter."

I have touched on some well-known peculiarities of Mormonism in this chapter. If I were to write of all the oddities

I know of the religion, I could easily fill a volume. In fact, more than a handful of historians have done just that. The Church has a difficult task in front of them in their efforts to become more mainstream Christian. Church documents and historical records are easily found in books and online. It's nearly impossible for the Mormon Church to hide from its past.

When I was growing up, church members and the hierarchy took pride in the ideas and practices that were peculiar to Mormonism. Those days are gone.

STAGE TWO
Mythical-Literal Faith

CHAPTER 3

Tell Me A Story

To hell with facts! We need stories!

-Ken Kesey

About the time children start school, they begin to see the world in a more logical fashion. Generally, they accept the stories told to them by their parents and their religious leaders and they view these stories quite literally. Narratives begin to build during this stage and children start to understand the rules, both implied and inferred, of their family.

Among the hallmarks of Stage 2 are order, dependability, fairness and reciprocity. There is an emergence of story and one-dimensional interpretation of symbols. In the case of order and dependability, a child begins to understand ideas and behaviors that are consistent.[33] Little Samantha, upon hearing her father use an expletive while driving may say, "Daddy, you just said a bad word." Using the same word in a different context, say to express gratitude, "That was awfully damn nice of them to pick up the garbage," would elicit the same kind of response from Samantha, who lacks the ability to discern contrasting contexts. She depends on the notion that "damn" is always a bad word, no matter who uses it and no matter the circumstances around its use.

I was taught very early in church that smoking and drinking alcohol, coffee or tea were "bad" as they violated the Word of Wisdom, as indicated in the *Doctrine and Covenants,*[34] one of Mormonism's canonical bodies of scripture. Neither my parents, nor my grandparents smoked or drank any of the forbidden beverages, at least not that I was aware of.

When I was a young child, I recall going to a neighbor's house just as my friend finished her lunch. She had a sandwich, but what caught my attention was the cola she was given to drink (until recently, colas were forbidden, at least for some of the more literally-minded members). I didn't verbalize my thoughts, but I considered that drink to be very bad. I felt a bit nervous being in the presence of a parent who would allow their child to drink cola. I was clear, even then, that it was the parent who was at fault and not necessarily the child.

Smoking was especially bad. I don't think it was ever expressed to me that smokers themselves were bad, but I interpreted smokers this way. They were at best suspect and at worst, downright evil.

These early childhood implantations stayed with me well into adulthood and years after I became a coffee and cocktail drinker myself. Whenever I saw someone drinking one of the prohibited beverages or smoking a cigarette, I would have a knee-jerk reactive thought that they were bad people. I did not discern between the behavior and the person. If you did bad things then you were bad. I judged myself by this standard for decades. But what is "bad" is subjective. My only frame of reference for a very long time was the Church. It was easy to see how this view of behavior transferred over.

Throughout much of my life, when I crossed the invisible line of appropriate behavior for an observant Mormon, I subconsciously, and sometimes consciously, deemed myself as bad which developed into overwhelming shame. It took me many years and a lot of work to overcome the soul-killing shame that permeated my life.

During the second stage of faith, reciprocity and fairness actually go hand-in-hand. It's the concept that if I do someone a favor, they owe me a favor in return. For example, if I share my candy with my little brother, then I expect him to share something of his with me.

A sense of fairness comes into play with Stage 2. It's the expectation that if my teacher gave *you* a stick of gum, she must give me one as well. When seven-year-old Curtis says, "That isn't fair!" it usually means that another person received a treat or was allowed a privilege that Curtis was not. Again, there is no contextual concept taken into consideration as to the fairness of the treatment. It's an either/or way of viewing reality.

The emergence of story or personal narrative begins during Stage 2. Someone outside of me, a parent, teacher, bishop, or deity, makes rules and I follow them without question. By taking on ourselves the beliefs and stories given to us by these authoritative figures, we make sense of our own world. Symbols take on a literal or one-dimensional meaning. Sometimes the literal meaning is the one that is supposed to stick throughout one's life, for example, the anthropomorphic view of God (ascribing human characteristics and form to deity). Even adults are taught that the Mormon God (separate from Jesus) is made up of flesh and bone, "The Father has a body of flesh and bones as tangible as man's."[35]

While the majority of people naturally transition out of Stage 2 when they become teenagers, there are a few who stay there throughout their adult lives.

CHAPTER 4

DNA Mormon

The family is central to the Creator's plan for the
eternal destiny of His children.[36]
>   -The Family: A Proclamation to the World

If there's such a thing as a DNA Mormon then that is how
I would described myself. My parents and their parents
before them were staunch Latter Day Saints. I come from six
generations of pioneer roots that run deep in both my maternal
and paternal bloodlines.

On my father's side, my great-grandparents, Andrew
Peterson and Anna Maria converted to Mormonism while
still in Sweden. They were the only ones in their families to
convert. They left their homeland in 1862 for America by
way of Germany. They were a couple by then, but not yet
married. Because of the long journey ahead of them, the captain
of the ship suggested (I suspect rather strongly in order to
prevent couples from succumbing to carnal temptation), that
all unmarried couples should marry. Consequently, my great-
grandparents were married onboard the ship. Eventually they
would end up in Lehi, Utah, south of Salt Lake City, where they
settled and produced ten children. Joseph, my father's father
was the third.

As far as I can tell, polygamy was never practiced by any of my grandfather Peterson's family. While plural marriage was being practiced at the time, my great grandmother, Mary Ann (which was her Americanized name), was not open to that possibility. I admire that tenacity in her and like to think I may have inherited some of it.

My earliest known ancestor in my paternal grandmother's line was John Savage born in England, 1733. As an adult, he sailed to America with the British Army but eventually deserted. He and his red-haired Irish wife, whose name is not known, had a son, Daniel Savage. Once grown, Daniel Savage married Sally Parrish and together they had a son, Levi Savage.

When Levi grew to adulthood, he married Polly Haynes. Levi, Polly, and their children converted to Mormonism in 1843. Unfortunately, Polly died several years later. Their second child was named after his father. He became known as Levi Savage Junior and would become my great-great-grandfather. Soon after Polly's death, Levi Savage *Senior* journeyed west with the Saints arriving in Salt Lake in September 1847, only two months after Brigham Young's group arrived on July 24th.

Polly and Levi's son, Levi Jr. proved to be a rather interesting family member. Much can be said for the records left behind by my ancestors. Even today, Church members are encouraged to keep detailed, albeit faith-promoting, journals for their own progeny. But the stories I remember best are those told to me by my father and grandmother. I will use both sources to briefly recount what is known about Levi Jr.

As a young man in his early twenties, Levi Jr. joined the Mormon Battalion (a religiously-based unit of the U.S. Military). As such, he played a part in the Mexican War. When he returned to Utah, having marched with the Battalion in Santa Fe, Tucson, and other areas, he married Jane Mathers, my great-great-grandmother. The year was 1848. Jane's story is the one I remember the most. It obviously touched my father deeply and by contagion, touched me too.

Jane converted to Mormonism as a teenager, which makes this account all the more poignant. At seventeen years old, she left her family home in Michigan to join the Saints in Nauvoo, Illinois. As she was walking away from her childhood home, a little sister, maybe only six years old, called her name, "Jane, Jane, Jane," as she ran out to her older sibling. Jane picked up her little sister and hugged her one last time before setting her down and directing her to go back home. It was the last time they would ever see one another. Jane never saw her birth family again. She was committed to her faith in Mormonism and left her kin to follow the Saints.

A common motif emerged in journals and accounts of my ancestors, and I suppose of many early Mormons, and that was the suffering they endured by becoming members of The Church of Jesus Christ of Latter Day Saints. All accounts at my disposal were told in the context of the Church. Therefore, baptism dates were perhaps as important, if not more so, as actual birth dates. Story after story detailed the sacrifices made and the enduring fortitude required to survive the unsurvivable. In the long run, it only strengthened the individual's faith in the Church and served as a reminder to the generations that followed that we must not take for granted the blood, sweat, and tears shed by our forebears for the "one true church."

Before Jane Mathers married my great-great-grandfather, she married a man, Milo Webb, as a second wife. Her sister wife (multiple wives belonging to the same husband) treated her poorly and Jane left her husband and journeyed west with Levi Savage *Senior* serving as a cook and camp hand.

Once married to Levi Jr., Jane gave birth to a son, Levi Mathers Savage, my paternal grandmother's father. Only a few short years later, Jane died. I see Jane as both a faithful adherent and also as a tragedy. No doubt, she displayed an amazing amount of strength and courage. She was a woman of faith and vaulting determination. But, because of my own doubts in Mormonism, I am saddened by the losses she endured, particularly the loss of her birth family.

Great-great-grandmother Jane Mathers died in 1851. In 1852, Brigham Young, the second Prophet, Seer, and Revelator of the Church, called the widower, Levi Jr., on a mission to Siam (current day Thailand). In the early years of the Church it was not unusual for married men or men with children to be called on missions, thereby leaving their families—sometimes for years. This mission was the beginning of a journey for my great-great-grandfather that included circumnavigating the globe and an ill-fated trek west that cost over two hundred Saints their lives.

Leaving his young son, Levi Mathers, with a sister, Levi Jr. sailed to India. From there he went to Rangoon. I remember well my father telling the story of Levi being in a ship sailing toward Siam when the vessel hit an electrical storm on the high seas. It generated an atmospheric electric field, a natural phenomenon known as St. Elmo's Fire. This caused the ship's mast to light up with an eerie blue/green glow. As a pilot in the Air Force, my own father experienced this anomaly while flying through lightning storms. The rim around the aircraft's windshield took on the same luminous glow that Levi Jr. experienced on the ship.

Levi Savage Jr. never made it to Siam and he did not convert a single person to Mormonism during his four years away. When he arrived back in America, he joined up with another group of Mormon Saints as they were getting ready to head west to Salt Lake. They would use hand-carts rather than wagons. Levi

Jr. advised them not to go as it was too late in the season. The Willie and Martin Handcart Companies, by which the groups were known, chose to go anyway. In an ill-fated but informed decision, Levi chose to travel with the group.

The companies were ravaged by snow and bitter cold winds. Livestock died and many of the Saints froze to death or died of hunger. I remember a popular image that depicted a cold, bitter landscape and a shallow grave. In the grave was a blanket-wrapped corpse. Looking down at the body was a forlorn woman, holding an infant, grief stricken at the death of this loved one.[37] Much has been written about the Willie and Martin Handcart tragedy and I will discuss it in more detail in a later chapter.

Levi Jr. eventually married one of the surviving members of the Willie Handcart Company, a widow who had two daughters. When the two girls grew older, Levi married them, too. Because of his practice of polygamy, which was against federal law, Levi served a prison sentence in the penitentiary convicted of illegal cohabitation. The last decades of his life were a sharp contrast to the first ones. He settled in Toquerville, Utah and eked out a living by farming. He died in December 1910 and was buried in the Toquerville cemetery.

Levi's oldest son, Levi Mathers Savage, my great-grandfather, married a woman named Marintha Wright. Wilford Woodruff, an apostle at the time, but eventually would serve as the fourth president of The Church of Jesus Christ of Latter Day Saints, convinced Levi Mathers that living the law of celestial marriage as outlined in *The Doctrine and Covenants*, would be an honorable thing to do.[38] Marintha would have none of it. When Levi Mathers married my great-grandmother, Lydia Lenora (Nora) Hatch, Marintha took her three children and left him. Not long after, Levi married Nora's younger sister, Hannah

Adeline Hatch. He lived his life with these two wives and as far as I know, never saw Marintha and their children again.

Great-Grandpa, in order to escape federal prosecution for illegal cohabitation, lived in Mexico for a time. He eventually returned to the States and settled in Northern Arizona in a desolate, windy town known as Woodruff that sat on top of a bluff. He served as Bishop for their ward (local congregation similar to a Catholic parish) for twenty-six years and when he left Woodruff exclaimed he never wanted to set foot in it again. He died at the age of eighty-three in Salt Lake City and is buried there next to his second wife, my great-grandmother, Nora.

My mother's family was equally entrenched in Mormonism. My maternal great-great-grandfather, Barnard White, newly converted to the Church, left London, England as a fifteen year old boy in 1855. He was alone, but his mother and sisters soon followed. They joined him in Boston and migrated west eventually settling in Ogden, Utah. Barnard lived a polygamous life. His daughter, Ada White Harding, was my great-grandmother Harding whom I vaguely remember visiting when she was bed-ridden. She died when I was a small child so my memories are spotty at best. My nineteenth century ancestors heralded Mormonism into the twentieth century, where it has carried on ever since.

Even though I have left the faith, in a very real sense Mormonism runs through my veins; it is in my genetic code. If you cut me, I would bleed Mormonism, at least in part. It doesn't matter whether one wants to leave the faith or not. Intellectually and spiritually, we do what we must. But on the most visceral level imaginable, Mormonism is there in the recesses of my psyche. As much as I want to "leave it alone," I can't. It keeps hammering at my gut, my mind, my heart. In truth, it won't leave *me* alone. The major journey of my life was leaving a religion so immensely ingrained in the most basic molecular structure of my being, that to deny its presence is to deny a very essential thread of who I am today.

It wasn't until I was in my fifties that I would realize that I needed to embrace the reality of my past if I wanted to step into the mystical stage of faith. Until then, I had a long arduous journey ahead of me.

STAGE THREE

Synthetic-
Conventional Faith

CHAPTER 5

I Know the Church Is True

It is both the duty and privilege of the Latter-day
Saints to know that their religion is true.[39]

-Brigham Young

The characteristics of Stages 1 and 2 really belong in the life of a child. By the time a person reaches adolescence, however, their lives have expanded beyond their family. They have school, friends, and sometimes work. They begin to see themselves within the context of an all-encompassing belief system that they belong to and identify with.

Within the tradition of Mormonism, the child has already been baptized and confirmed a member of the Church. This happens at age eight, generally. They identify themselves as Mormon or LDS and if they are regular churchgoers, they know that the first sacrament meeting of the month is reserved for members to bear their testimonies as to the truthfulness of the gospel. This monthly service is called fast and testimony meeting, as members are supposed to fast for two meals that day. Even young members are encouraged to bear their testimonies. Until quite recently, small children, sometimes as young as three, were urged by parents to stand up and with microphone in hand speak the words whispered into their ear by a parent,

"I know the church is true. I know Joseph Smith is a prophet of God. . . ."

Characteristic of this stage is a reliance on the authorities of the Church. There is an understanding or assumption that Church leaders know the will of God and correctly impart that understanding onto the members who are compliant, some more than others.

The devoutly religious individual may not have the ability to think outside of the confines of their specific world view. Quoting Santayana, James Fowler writes, "We don't know who discovered water but we know it wasn't the fish."[40] A Stage 3 person is like the fish that cannot see the water in which it is immersed.

Conversely, Fowler states that entering Stage 4 (when we begin to question previously held notions) would be the equivalent of the fish jumping out of the fish tank and beginning to reflect upon the water or when members begin to see the world with a new perspective and can critically evaluate their old ideas.

People in Stage 3 may be aware that there are other traditions but may not necessarily know much about them. They have a certainty in their beliefs that answer life's most complex questions. It's a pleasant place to be because you "know" who you are and where you're going. You have a strong sense of belonging to *your* tribe.

I'm reminded of a former student who had gotten married in the Mormon temple and was now allowed to wear the sacred garments (underwear). I always thought they were an unattractive and uncomfortable requirement for men and women, but mostly for women. They were hot, unflattering and confining. But Charlotte was excited to be part of the tribe. It never dawned on me until then that anyone could be anything but disappointed and resigned to wearing the garments. For Charlotte, they were a symbol of her spiritual progress and added a sacred dimension to her life. But ultimately, it was a sign that she belonged, she was part of the in-group. Psychologically speaking, it's a vital part of maturing to adulthood and Abraham Maslow ranks the hierarchal need for belonging at number three out of five.

For the most part, Stage 3ers are content to be where they are because, quite frankly, they are not aware of what they don't know and what they do know they like. They often have no reason to question or to search out an alternative worldview. Because of this, they may not have given much time to seriously critique their tradition's teachings. A familiar statement written by General Authority Ezra Taft Benson (who would eventually become the thirteenth president of the Church), wraps up this idea, "When our leaders speak, the thinking has been done."[41]

A characteristic answer to such questions as, "What do you think about R-rated films?" might elicit a response like, "Well, the Church's position is . . . ." or "The prophet says. . ."

One semester, while teaching a college writing class, I had an incident that reflected the commitment to obedience that many exhibit in Stage 3. One of the essays I assigned was a film analysis. I chose *The Color Purple*, rated PG-13. Because this was a college class, all my students were adults eighteen years old or older. I could have chosen an R-rated film, but since this college was in Utah, I chose PG-13 because I was well-aware that many Mormons, even adult members heeded the suggestion to avoid viewing films with an R-rating,

> It is a concern that some of our young Latter-day Saints, as well as their parents, regularly watch R-rated and other inappropriate movies and videos. One more reason why the devil laugheth, and his angels rejoice (3 Ne. 9:2).[42]

Admittedly I was bothered by this request from the church hierarchy as I was outspoken when it came to censorship and, in fact, had chosen censorship as the theme for a particular writing course. During the semester we studied the First Amendment to the Constitution of the United States and read books that directly related to this issue including *Fahrenheit 451* by Ray Bradbury and *Reading Lolita in Tehran* by Azir Nafisi. As a requirement, my students were to read a book of their choice that had either been challenged or banned. I was passionate about First Amendment issues, but I was also respectful of the community views—or so I thought.

The day I announced to my class what film we would be viewing, I had three students stay after to talk with me. They could not watch the film, they told me, because they made a commitment to themselves not to watch PG-13 films. "What," I asked them, "do you imagine is in a PG-13 film?" They did not answer my question directly. They just repeated, "We've made a commitment not to watch PG-13 films." One of the students said she could get an edited version of the film so they could all watch it at her home. I told them to do as they wish, but I would not give them deferential treatment when it came to grading their essays. They agreed and it was settled, but not for me. I was troubled that three adults had refused to view a film—not a raunchy film, but one made in good taste with a powerful message.

I had studied totalitarian governments for years as a teacher and debate coach. I had read countless books about the harmful effects of censorship and I was greatly disturbed by the increasing trend I was seeing where adults would not trust their own judgments for fear they might lose control of their moral abilities if they allowed ideas to creep into their minds. They were behaving with the mentality of an adolescent who could not be trusted to control his or her own base impulses so they must have someone do it for them.

This was a dangerous precedent, I thought. I did not sleep well that night or the night after that. As an instructor, I knew I couldn't let this go. I was determined to express my concerns with my students. At our next meeting, I began class with a speech where I passionately discussed the dangers of censorship, citing specific examples.

People, every day, all over the planet were breaking the laws of censorship set forth by their governments and religions in order to read and to watch what they knew should be a basic human right. I told them that the first sign of the deterioration of an individual's rights was when they chose to self-censor as a result of an authority figure. Censorship, I continued, is dangerous to a democracy. I went on for twenty minutes reminding them of passages we'd read and court cases we had analyzed.

After class, a line of about eight students formed, each one telling me in their own words that they appreciated what I had to say. Unfortunately, the three students who had come to me earlier were not there to hear me. Furthermore, two additional students had joined them. However, the word must have gotten out because at the next class meeting all but two of my students were present and remained so throughout the viewing of the film.

Religious institutions, in order to survive, must insist that their adherents maintain the rules and structures set forth by that particular tradition. If you have a church filled with radical people with opposing views, then the institution will inevitably fail. Rules and mandates are put into place to keep members from questioning. Using a reward and punishment system is one way to achieve control over members. In his book, *Eternal Life*, John Shelby Spong, a retired Episcopal priest, writes, "Ideas that have nothing to do with life after death, but everything to do with controlling human behavior in the here and now, are simply not worthy of human beings, religious or otherwise."[43]

Regardless of the religious institution, if an individual is to grow along spiritual lines, to fully embrace what it means to be human, if they are to transition into Stage 4, they *must* begin to question. This usually begins when a person leaves home or goes away to college and out into the world of ideas. It's when they discover that there are other world-views and some of them make a lot of sense. The certainty that a person once held onto firmly now begins to crack.

A common metaphor used by doubting Mormons is a shelf. Uncertainties arise and the believing Mormon puts them on the shelf—the metaphorical back burner of the mind. They decide to go the extra mile in preparing for their Gospel Doctrine lesson and during the course of their online research they read bits and pieces of disturbing historical facts. Plop—onto the shelf they go. To rid themselves of the increasing cognitive dissonance they're experiencing, they decide to read faith promoting books to heal the cracks in their Mormon armor. But they find when reading the *Journal of Discourses* and *History of the Church*, that there are even more inconsistencies and unsettling teachings from prophets, such as Brigham Young. And then they begin to wonder why they were never told about these things before. In fact, the active Latter Day Saint may begin to see a pattern of deception being perpetuated by the Church where it's not just a matter of omitting certain facts, but that there is a concerted effort to misrepresent details or to flat out deny their existence.

More doubts may come to the member's awareness, sometimes a little bit of anger creeps in alongside it. That shelf is starting to bow. The doubter commits to being more diligent about reading their scriptures and bearing their testimony. But in a conscientious effort to strengthen their testimony by reading the 1830 edition of *The Book of Mormon*, they inadvertently run across the changes—and they are significant—between that version and the one they bought two years ago. If too many bits of information and knowledge are piled on this shelf, it eventually cracks before it breaks down completely. This may look like a bad thing, but it's not. One cannot move forward in their faith without the sacrament of doubt.

It doesn't matter what your intellectual development is, either. It's all about faith. This explains why someone of superior intellectual prowess may still stay within Stage 3 of faith for the duration of their life. While growing along the intellectual or cognitive stages, they are, nevertheless, stunted in terms of their faith. It reminds me of Sheldon Cooper, one of the main characters in the television sitcom *The Big Bang Theory*. Sheldon is considered a genius in terms of his intellectual ability. He is a theoretical physicist working at Caltech in Pasadena. But when it comes to social development—how he interacts with others— he is inept. Even he recognizes this and often asks his buddy, Leonard, for clarification when a suspected sarcastic comment is hurled his way.

If we replace the social stages with faith stages, then it's clear what point I'm making. Unfortunately, the intellectual Mormon may begin to sense the "danger" of doubt and quickly retreat never to open that Pandora's Box again. But if you are reading this book, then chances are, you've flung the lid wide open and all hell is breaking loose!

Chapter 6

A Borrowed Testimony

Do not believe on the strength of traditions even if they have been held in honor for many generations and in many places. . . After investigation, believe that which you have yourselves tested and found reasonable, and which is for your good and that of others.[44]

-Buddha

I loved Sunday school as a young girl. I would take special care putting on my church clothes, always feeling especially pretty when I did. I remember sitting in the basement room of the old church house as my Sunday school teacher held up a picture of Joseph Smith, the founder, and talked about the First Vision. I thought Smith was very handsome. He was no less than a god to me then. I believed all I was told; what eight-year-old wouldn't believe the adults in her life?

I was fascinated with the supernatural tales of angels and God and Jesus appearing before the young Joseph. My teachers bore their testimonies, their spiritual witness given to them by the Holy Ghost, that the Church was true and that Joseph Smith was a prophet of God. They told us that we, too, could gain a testimony to the truthfulness of Mormonism by obeying the commandments, reading the Mormon scriptures, and following the prophet. We would know by a "burning of the bosom," the truth of all they were teaching us.

I believed that I would experience my own spiritual witness that the Church was true. I would have to be baptized first followed by the laying on of hands by worthy priesthood holders so that I may receive the gift of the Holy Ghost, who would be a constant companion to me provided I follow the gospel. I was warned however, that the Holy Ghost would leave me if I was to ever doubt the truthfulness of Mormonism. The very idea sent me reeling in fear.

In the Mormon Church, children are baptized at eight years old–the age of accountability. The baptism can take place at an older age for converts to the Church, but never at a younger one. In the first years of Sunday school, much of the time is spent preparing children for baptism by immersion, which is required of all members.

I looked forward to this pivotal event. I knew it meant I would be cleansed of all my sins. And I had committed many sins from lying to stealing money from my mother's red wallet, to using an occasional "hell." I was a flawed human being; I knew that already. I was innately bad. My baptism would be my moment of complete redemption. I promised myself that I would not commit another sin once I was baptized, a promise that I would break before the week was up.

I wanted nothing less than rebirth. What I got was a confirmation that I was a flawed individual. I lied; I cheated; I stole; I broke my fast on Fast Sunday, probably no more or no less than any other child, but I didn't know that. I talked too much in school and was criticized by my teachers. No matter, I loved my classmates and sensed they loved me too. I was loud, boisterous, funny, and yes, I was peculiar.

I loved being the center of attention. But under the facade of frivolity was the knowledge that I was not lovable. If they knew the real Erin, the one who committed sin after sin, they would turn in disgust. So I couldn't let them see who I really was. When feelings of loneliness, inadequacy, and self-hatred oozed up from my viscera, I would promptly push them down with food—bread, cookies, ice cream, anything that would stuff them down just far enough to be out of reach. From eight years old, I began using food as a salve, a nurturer that asked for nothing in return. If unconditional love and acceptance was not demonstrative in my life, food was. I became overweight. Not a lot, perhaps, but enough that I found something else to beat myself up over.

I learned that my salvation depended on my good works. I wanted to be good, but goodness eluded me! I did believe, however. It's not that I necessarily trusted the Church, but I did trust the authority figures in my life. I could trust that they knew what they were talking about. And I had no doubt that when they said, "I know the Church is true," that they *really* meant it. But I struggled with what I saw as my inner demons. I grew to hate the person I thought I was. I was ugly, fat, and stupid. I was always making mistakes and I was unlovable. Along with self-hatred, there was fear which played a major role in my childhood.

The notion of the Second Coming of Christ was prominent in my growing up years. I was taught that the Millennium would be the beginning of a thousand year reign in which the righteous would be saved and the unrighteous would be destroyed.

Regardless of what side you belonged, the world would be a scary place. Brother would fight brother. Those who didn't plan ahead would rob the food and medical supplies of those who had. And the Saints would be beckoned to Jackson County Missouri, where the Garden of Eden had really existed. It was there that Christ would appear before the Latter Day Saints who were the only ones blessed with the fullness of the restored gospel. In fact, I was told, the Church was in the process of building apartments in that area of Missouri so we would have lodging once we arrived—by foot. You see trains, planes and automobiles and the fuel to source them would not be available to us. We would take little else but the clothes on our backs, much like our pioneer ancestors.

I was, in fact, a very fearful child. I would become so frightened that I would enter into a state of surrealism. Whatever chemicals were released in my body caused me to experience an almost dreadful sensation of floating away from the reality I knew. At these times of intense terror, I found it hard to swallow and feared I would choke to death. Whether sitting in my third grade class or practicing our Christmas Carols in the school auditorium, I would remember the Millennium and a colossal wave of fear would sweep over my entire being and that same "out of reality" feeling would consume me. The only solace I found was the reassurance that I may live a long life and perhaps as an adult, the fear would magically disappear.

There was talk, although it wasn't in Mormon scripture, that at the turn of the century, Christ would return. But it could happen before as well. I would calculate in my head how old I would be in the year 2000, 'Let's see, I'll be forty-two years old. That's pretty old. Maybe by then, I won't be scared anymore.'

There were nights when the moon took on an orange or reddish hue and I would immediately think of the phrase, "And the moon shall turn to blood." A shot of dread stabbed through my gut, my breathing increased, and I slipped out of reality, once again, thinking that this might be it. No doubt I was afraid to die, for eternity was something so incomprehensible to me that I simply could not deal with it in my present state of consciousness.

During my seventh and eighth grade years I took a painting class in a town about a thirty minute drive away. Riding home from painting lessons, particularly in the winter when it was dark outside by 6:00 P.M., I would look up at the moon for any signs of scarlet. At times I wasn't sure. It was, perhaps, red enough to ignite another episode within. Most nights the moon merely told me I had another day without worry.

In the end, I wanted to believe the Church to be true because my parents believed and so did the parents of my friends and all the Church leaders. I had long ago stopped trusting my own internal marching orders. When I acted upon them, I was reprimanded. I learned quickly that I could not trust myself and so I vested all trust onto others. Do what they say, and I would be fine. But I was not fine. I wanted so much to have that "burning of the bosom" that they all spoke of, an assurance in my heart that what I was learning was true, but it simply would not come. And then I entered my teens.

My teen years were filled with rebellious behavior and reacting against authority figures. I detested attending church, but I didn't have a choice in the matter. It seemed to me that the Church meant more in the lives of the members than their own family members. Yet they extolled the importance and strength of eternal families. I was unimpressed. Even so, I always believed that I would sow my oats now and eventually calm down once I married and had a family. Then I would settle into a respectable Mormon life. I would feel different then; of that I was certain. Maybe I would finally grasp onto the elusive testimony that I still had not captured. But until then, I would do as I wanted—at least what I could get away with. That didn't last long. At sixteen I became pregnant and "had to get married." I was as ready for married life and motherhood as any sixteen-year-old and it was a tough go for a long time.

In terms of background and family life, my husband and I were well suited for each other. He, too, grew up in a respectable Mormon home just a few miles from where my family lived. When we first married, we tried attending church a couple of times but found we much rather enjoyed our Sundays at home or in an outdoor activity. Deep inside, we both figured we would eventually do what was expected of us and go through the temple after our one year waiting period—a requirement for situations like ours where sin was a factor.

When the year was up, my husband and I readied ourselves so we could obtain a temple recommend, a card that indicated the holder had successfully passed their worthiness interview and could enter into the House of the Lord. On June 22, 1976, my husband and I entered into the Ogden temple to complete our endowments and to be sealed to one another and our seven-month-old son for time and all eternity.

While there, we each received a secret name. Before the end of the session, my husband would know mine. I would never know his. When it came time for the ritual of "going through the veil," it was God who called my husband, who was a priesthood holder, to enter into the Celestial Kingdom. It was my husband who called me, by my new name, into the highest degree of glory. Bottom line, I was dependent on the priesthood that only a man could hold, to secure my place into heaven. This did not set well with me. Nor did it set well with my husband.

We both left the temple in shock at the graphically violent pantomime, frightening oaths, and rituals, including putting on the sacred underwear, the garments, that temple-worthy Mormons are instructed to wear at all times. What we took part in that day left us with a disturbing feeling that we had just joined a cult. Since members vow not to talk about what goes on inside the temples because of the sacred nature, we did not know what to expect beforehand.

Going through the temple was the beginning of the end for me. I wanted to believe, I really did. But I knew that what I had just experienced was not holy—at least not for me. But then I could not be trusted. I was confused and entered into a state of limbo for a time. That changed several years later when I would, once again, try becoming active in the Church.

CHAPTER 7

Glimpses of Sunlight

You're bound to get idears if you go thinkin' about stuff.[45]

-The Grapes of Wrath by John Steinbeck

I began my college career at age twenty-five, when my youngest son began kindergarten. This allowed me half a day and evenings for my studies. I had always planned on attending college–I knew I would, but getting pregnant and married at sixteen curtailed that plan for a few years. By the time I began attending my first quarter of college, I was passionate about this new phase of life, passionate and a bit nervous.

My relationship with Mormonism was shifting. My husband and I had been active members for a year or so, feeling a sense of obligation and quite a bit of guilt for staying away as long as we had. We now had two children and felt that we owed them a stable upbringing that, in our world, meant taking them to Sunday school to ready them for baptism.

I still had not acquired the much desired testimony that the restored gospel was true. I was frustrated about this and perplexed that what seemed to come so easily for everyone else, eluded me. I've since wondered if all the people I believed had testimonies really did. Mormonism was (and still is) a works-for-salvation based religion, with pride as its cornerstone. To properly fit in, one had to have the appearance of a testimony, of a life in alignment with the ideals of Mormonism. Outward appearances were a crucial component to being a member in good standing. Members denied that something as superficial as external appearances was important, but it was an unspoken cultural phenomenon, nevertheless.

I grew close to many of the members in my ward (the local congregation) who were at the same stage in life as me—raising a young family. In fact, my deep feelings for these people kept me in the Church longer than I should have stayed. When I think of my friends from this time, it's always with the utmost respect and love. One particular friend, who was also my jogging partner, had been the catalyst for my enrollment at the local university. She was a student and we spent our morning jogs talking about Shakespeare and other works she was studying at the University. I was intellectually stimulated by our early morning conversations and wanted more of the same.

In my first quarter of college I took three classes, American History, Philosophy 101, and an introductory literature course. I did not realized how absolutely barren my mind was until I began my studies. I could not get enough. My brain was a dry sponge being dipped into a sea of ideas and it felt invigorating. When possible, I sat on the front row in all my classes to ensure I would hear every last word uttered by the professor.

Plato's works were required reading for my philosophy class. It was while reading Plato that my mind experienced a detectable perception shift. I was especially intrigued by his Allegory of the Cave and I often referred to it with my own students when I taught high school and college later on.

Plato's Allegory described a group of people chained to the wall of a cave. They've spent their entire lives facing the back wall. Between the group and the outside activities was a large fire that caused shadows to be cast on the interior cave wall. The group observed muted figures at the back of the cave and assumed the shadows were reality. The sounds they heard were only echoes of sounds from outside.

The chains prevented the prisoners from turning around so they had no way of realizing that what they were seeing were only imitations of the real thing. Because they knew nothing different, they were satisfied with "reality" as they knew it. If someone actually left the cave and went out into the sunlight, they were blinded at first by the intensity of the light, which represented knowledge. Once that person grew accustomed to it, they realized that what they previously perceived as truth was, in fact, merely a shadow of reality.[46]

The people in the cave lived in a world of ignorance, but they were satisfied because they knew no other life. I saw it was the same with my own life and those around me. When many of us first started to gain knowledge, we became frightened and ran back to our old ways of thinking. But when we continued to seek knowledge and truth, we came to embrace it. A risk we took was that others often viewed us as bizarre—sometimes even evil.

In addition to Plato, we were required to read *The World's Religions* by Huston Smith. It covered both Western and Eastern traditions. I was particularly intrigued with Buddhism; but frankly, they all fascinated me. I began to step outside my cave and see the sunlight for the first time and I liked what I saw. I received more questions than answers which started a pursuit for knowledge that I've yet to tire of. I began to believe Socrates' words, "The only true wisdom is in knowing you know nothing." Being a seeker became my new passion, so "not knowing" was a welcome realization.

I wondered what other ideas were out there that I hadn't yet explored. I found myself delving into all sorts of esoteric literature that up until that time was forbidden. Now, nothing was off limits. Over the next few years, that sense of awe and potentiality of the Beginner's Mind[47] was with me in most of my waking moments. I could explore anything! What had previously been taboo topics, forbidden to think about let alone utter, became available to me. I looked at reincarnation, space warps, quantum mechanics and vertical time, where all events occurred simultaneously only in different dimensions. I found quantum entanglement, what Einstein called "spooky action at a distance," to be especially intriguing.

I was excited at the endless possibilities. But it was more than that. With new eyes, I began to critically evaluate all previously held notions and beliefs. Was Mormonism really true? What about God? Was He really a he? Did a god even exist? Or was God closer to what Einstein believed—more of an energy field?

The first time I heard about the divine spark that existed within each of us was, oddly enough, during a discussion in my English Romantic literature class. The professor took his chalk and ground one end of it in the middle of the chalkboard, leaving a dot.

"This dot," he explained, "represents the divine spark that's in all of us." He went on to explain how many of the Romantics were in touch with that spark and developed it in their writings. He spoke of Einstein, saying something along the lines that Einstein had reasoned the Theory of Relativity up to a point and then he followed a light beam.

Basically, what he was saying and what I learned since then from my own experience was that our rational, linear minds could do amazing things. They could take us far, but they had their limits. Once we reached the limits of our physical brains, there was another source into which we could tap, the Ground of Being that had no limits and had an inexhaustible number of possibilities.

It was in this field of Divine Energy, that Einstein perceived what he could not comprehend with his mind alone. This field was where writers such as Coleridge, Whitman, and Shakespeare and artists like Michelangelo, Van Gogh, and O'Keefe entered to birth a creative expression that could not be adequately explained in any other way. It was a field of energy that we all— everyone, every being that has lived or ever will live had access to if we merely learned how to tap into It.

These ideas came to me in the mid-1980's before the Internet. And while they had been around for millennia, these concepts were a new way of perception for the average American, and especially for the average Utah Mormon woman. It took me nearly thirty more years before I would take my intellectual understanding of these concepts to a heightened level.

Ideas were coming at me from all angles and I was in a tailspin of new thoughts. But then there was the matter of Mormonism. I remained active in the Church during my first two years of college and had been bumped up from counselor in the Primary (LDS children's organization) to President. I did well in this role as I was organized and enjoyed children. But something was askew. I was experiencing increasing cognitive dissonance. I still didn't have a testimony and with the ideas I was exploring, I was not bound to get one. My relationship with the Church had to be addressed and I wasn't sure how it could possibly turn out well.

CHAPTER 8

Exodus

What I have said I know to be true; but seeing you are to go forward, I will go with you, will help all I can, will work with you, will rest with you, and if necessary, will die with you. May God in his mercy bless and preserve us.[48]

-Levi Savage Jr.

Following Joseph Smith's death in June of 1844, there was contention among the Latter Day Saints. The members were split into two groups. One group wanted to go back to Mormonism without polygamy and the temple. The others, led by Brigham Young, wanted everything to stay intact, just as Joseph had left it, including polygamy and the temple rites.

Time was running out. The governor's commission wanted the Mormons to leave Nauvoo. Brigham Young determined that since the Saints had been abandoned by Illinois—even the United States, that they should go westward toward Mexican territory. The majority of the LDS followed Brigham, but Joseph's widow, Emma, did not. She, along with her son, Joseph Smith III, stayed behind. This faction eventually formed what would be known as the Reorganized Church of Jesus Christ Of Latter Day Saints (RLDS). Today it is called The Community of Christ.

Brother Brigham, as the early Saints called him, had an astute talent for organizing. He gathered three thousand of his followers, collected the necessary provisions and traveled some thirteen hundred miles, through bitter cold temperatures, over the plains, and through the desert finally arriving in the Promised Land, the Great Salt Lake basin. It was this exodus that labeled Brigham Young the American Moses.

Under Brigham Young's supervision, the Mormons left Illinois on February 4, 1846—in the middle of winter. They forged through ice and frozen rivers. Once they landed in Nebraska, the Mormons set up a camp—Winter Quarters—that served as a stopping point for future migrations where the pioneers planted crops, replenished their supplies, and gathered what strength was necessary to continue toward the Great Basin of Salt Lake. This route became known as The Mormon Trail and was used for twenty years afterward, until the Transcontinental Railroad was established in 1869.

Music and dancing helped the Saints endure the journey. Their songs were filled with an undying certainty that what they were doing and where they were going was the will of God. "Come, Come Ye Saints," (originally called, "All is Well") written in 1846, was known as the pioneer anthem.[49] I was taught that at their lowest points, the Saints would sing this hymn. We sang it often when I was a child—another reminder of the early plight of the Mormon pioneers—of my ancestors—of my people.

For nearly a year and a half, the Saints suffered terribly, some paid with their lives. It was a brutal journey. Mothers buried their children who had starved or frozen to death. People collapsed from mere exhaustion. But these were a chosen people whom God held in His favor. No price was too great for them. Finally, on July 24, 1847 the first Mormon pioneers arrived in

Utah's Great Salt Lake Valley. Later that year, in December, Brigham Young was finally declared Joseph Smith's successor as Church Prophet.

The Territory of Deseret was created in 1849 with Brigham Young as governor. The next year the federal government created the Territory of Utah and appointed Young Territorial governor.[50]

When Brigham Young set out on this journey it was with the intention of finding a dwelling place where the LDS could live as they saw fit without government interference. All this changed with the development of Utah Territory.

Following their exodus from the East to the Great Basin, the Mormons increased their missionary efforts overseas. During this time, many people converted to the faith, especially in England, Wales, and the Scandinavian countries. The new converts were encouraged to travel to America and settle in the new Zion. Most of those who migrated from Europe had very little money and the move proved to be difficult. But Brigham Young set up the Perpetual Emigration Fund to provide financial support for people migrating to Utah.

By 1856, the Perpetual Emigration Fund had been depleted to the point that there just wasn't enough financial backing to cover the costs of oxen-pulled wagons. A more economical method was the use of handcarts to cross the rugged terrain into Salt Lake City.

Handcarts were significantly less costly than covered wagons. Instead of draft animals, the people themselves pulled the wheel-barrel-like carts on their own. Because the carts were considerably smaller than the oxen-drawn wagons used in earlier treks, fewer provisions could be taken. Adults were allowed seventeen pounds of personal belongings. A child was allowed ten pounds.[51]

Of the ten handcart companies that were to make the trek, all but two were successful. The treks of the Willie and Martin Handcart companies would end in tragedy.

My great-great-grandfather, Levi Savage Jr. played a pivotal role in the Willie Company. He had just returned from an unsuccessful mission toward Siam. It had been four years since he last saw his young son, Levi Mathers Savage, who had been living with a relative in Utah.

Levi Jr. joined up with the handcart group who was getting a late start because of unanticipated delays. The Willie Company left Iowa City, Iowa on July 15, 1856. The Martin Company left two weeks later on July 28. Levi warned them of the danger of leaving so late in the season and expressed his deep concern for the elderly people, women, and small children. He pleaded with the group to wait until spring, but the enthusiastic Saints, fervent in their belief that the Lord would watch over them and protect them in their journey, insisted on leaving despite the warning.[52]

In what was viewed as a courageous move on my grandfather's part and would dub him a hero of the Willie Handcart Company, Levi Savage Jr. is credited with saying the following, "What I have said I know to be true; but seeing you are to go forward, I will go with you, will help all I can, will work with you, will rest with you, and if necessary, will die with you. May God in his mercy bless and preserve us."[53]

There was speculation that these were not my grandfather's actual words as his journal entries depicted a more rugged vernacular. It was more common than not to portray a faith-promoting revision of history by expanding on the actual facts. The recent film version of this handcart trek, *17 Miracles* was an example of this point. It aimed to manipulate the viewers by evoking strong emotional responses, a persuasive technique that was used often and quite effectively. Nevertheless, Levi Savage realized the danger the Mormons would face and made the decision to risk his life by traveling with them. In the end, my grandfather made it to Salt Lake City. Many of the others did not.

Starting out their journey, they moved farther away from civilization with each day. It was an arduous march and most of the immigrants were former city dwellers from the old countries. Trekking hundreds of miles across the rugged American landscape was something they were not used to. On one particularly ominous day, they entered buffalo territory. A large herd of bison thundered toward the group who quickly moved their carts to make a path for the charging herd. In the confusion, the pioneers' own livestock were caught up in the stampede. The loss of their cattle and oxen was a foreshadowing of what still lay ahead.[54]

On October 8, 1856, Levi wrote, ". . . We traveled fifteen miles. Our old people are nearly all failing fast."[55]

October 15, in Sweet Water, Wyoming, he wrote that the group traveled in excess of fifteen miles. Seventeen-year-old Carline Reeder died during the night and was laid to rest in the morning. "The people are getting weak and failing fast. A great many are sick. . . Our rations were reduced last night, one quarter, bringing men to ten ounces and the women to nine ounces each."[56]

Their food rations continued being cut as their situation grew dire. At one point "Children chewed on bark, leaves, twigs, and the tattered leather from the boots of those who had died." The next night, there were three more deaths—and one birth.[57]

Because of their immense exhaustion, the pioneers needed to lighten their loads. They ended up burning what non-essentials they had, but they ended up burning some of their clothing and bedding as well. The women took over the pulling and pushing of the handcarts as so many of the men had exhausted their last reserve of energy and simply could not go on any longer.

On October 18, 1856 the pioneers crossed the Sweet Water River in Wyoming. The icy water soaked the emigrants clear through to their skin. Then came the snow—followed by the bitter wind. There were fourteen more deaths that night. Graves could not be dug because of the frozen ground, so the bodies were wrapped in blankets and laid out on the hard earth.

By October 18th and 19th, both the Willie and Martin Companies reached their breaking points. Earlier in the month, Brigham Young had been informed of the dismal situation and immediately sent relief for the emigrants. Assistance finally came on October 19th—too late for many, but for those still living, it was the help they had been desperately praying for. The children ate until their bellies were full. Levi Jr. reported in his journal that on that day of relief, three more people died including eight-year-old Daniel Osborn.[58]

Still the storms raged on and the death count rose. Mothers died. Children perished. "It was certainly heart rendering to hear children crying for mothers and mothers crying for children."

October 24, Friday, "This morning found us with thirteen corpses for burial. These were all put into one grave."

October 25 was Levi's final journal entry as he was too sick to record. ". . . I have not been able to keep a daily journal, but nothing much transpired, except the people died daily. . . "[59]

Finally, on November 9, 1856, the Willie Company arrived in Salt Lake City. The Martin Company arrived on November 30. In the end, over two hundred emigrants lost their lives in the Willie and Martin Handcart disaster, but over a thousand from the two groups arrived in Zion.

The stories of the treks westward are kept vividly alive as a reminder of what the early Mormons endured in order to practice their faith in peace. Today, throughout the western United States, Mormons re-enact the trek, donning pioneer clothing and using handcarts to carry their provisions. It's a way to bring home, firsthand, a small taste of what their pioneer ancestors endured.

The exodus westward was a harrowing tale of extraordinary suffering and courage. Part of my legacy and that of other descendants of the early pioneers is the continuation of grieving for our loved ones and the miserable trials they endured. We are duty-bound to honor them for their sacrifices. When I initially left the faith, I experienced guilt for my betrayal and carried it with me for many years.

STAGE FOUR

Individuative-
Reflective Faith

CHAPTER 9

Disentanglement

I distrust those people who know so well what
God wants them to do, because I notice it always
coincides with their own desires.

-Susan B. Anthony

Of all the stages, I view Stage 4 as the most difficult one.
I believe that Fowler's stage theory, for the most part,
pertains to this stage and this stage alone because in Stages
1, 2, and 3 individuals are perfectly happy with their current
state of consciousness. Stage theory is not relevant to Stages 5
and 6 because theories simply do not matter to people who have
reached these levels of spiritual understanding. But for those
of us in Stage 4, understanding the evolutionary process of the
stages of faith can mean the difference between life and death,
hopelessness and hopefulness, a world of darkness to a life of
exquisite harmony and grace.

All the stages are appropriate and necessary in their time; so
sidestepping this stage—going from Stage 3 to 5, cannot be done
as this process is evolutionary. We aren't able to enter Stage 5
without going through the unraveling of that which we held to be
true. This fourth stage is where our primary connection with our
Stage 3 group ends. It usually begins when a person enters college

or leaves their birth family's home. But if one is raised in a tradition that admonishes those who question, it may be years before an individual starts to explore. And many will remain in Stage 3 for their entire lives, never experiencing the holiness of dissent.[60]

Stage 4 people are concerned with authenticity—being true to themselves, even if they're not exactly sure what that means. But they may know what it *doesn't* mean. It is a rendering of sorts and it must be experienced in order for us to be in that place where awakening happens. No doubt, Stage 4 can be tear-filled. I think of tears as a means of cleansing. When we wash away the old with our tears, we are able to make room for the illumination that comes with Stage 5.

I found stage theory to be especially relevant because it gave me the light at the end of the tunnel. Before I became familiar with Fowler's work, I was tumbling around in the abyss and not certain it would ever come to an end. Understanding that these dark years actually led to something new and transcendent, helped me to hang on—to wait and hope. It motivated me to begin spiritual practices and to have the courage to go through my own break-through shadow process.

For me Stage 4 began at age twenty-five when I entered college. I was relatively young, but I've seen so many Mormons crash and burn when at age forty or fifty or even older, they explore ideas that do not reconcile with their Mormon beliefs. The effects can have devastating ramifications, including shattering one's identity, the dissolution of marriage and exile from extended and immediate family members.

Once a person begins to critically examine their own beliefs and that of others' they will often become disillusioned with their faith. What they once knew to be true, they now realize isn't, at least not in the way they had previously believed. They will oftentimes feel betrayed and angry.

So many of us who were once in the Church saw the myth of who we believed Joseph Smith was, begin to crumble and then to dissolve completely. Depending on the years devoted to believing the faith and the degree with which an individual believed and were committed, will determine the impact of the demythologizing or what I think of as the deconstruction process.

Many active Mormons believed wholeheartedly in the veracity of the Church and would have been willing to defend it with their life at any given moment if necessary. They devoted hours of service and thousands of dollars in tithing only to find out it was not what it presented itself to be.

The sense of betrayal is so profound that many former Mormons refuse to believe in anything along spiritual lines, ever again. Embracing atheism is not unusual. Atheism in itself is not a problem, rather it's the seething anger that so often accompanies it, when one feels like they've been duped their entire lives, that can be challenging.

If, like me, you find yourself steeped in rage, let me assure you that you're justified in your anger. We have a right to feel this way when we've been betrayed and have lost so much of our lives to building up what for us is now a false ideology. Think of all the hours away from family and friends and the goals you wanted to accomplish, but did not have the time to pursue because of the extraordinary amount of time required by the Church in order to maintain your active status. You have lost much, that is a given.

When I discovered for myself, that I could no longer stay in a tradition that so opposed my developing world-view, I began my long trek—not westward, like my ancestors, but inward toward a pathless land where I would be confronted with my own dragons that only I had the power to slay.

CHAPTER 10

Leaving the Tribe

Loyalty to a petrified opinion never yet broke a
chain or freed a human soul.

-Mark Twain

Like most Westerners, I belonged to a patriarchal religion.
As early as my teens male-dominated faith bothered me.
All authority figures were male. It's not that mothers and female
teachers didn't take me in their charge; they did. But ultimately,
all final decisions and certainly all decisions that really mattered
were determined by men. I tried to make sense of this but
couldn't. It wasn't just the Church, either. I grew up in an era
where this was the norm in American society.

Given the climate of 1960's America and adding into the mix
Mormonism, an exaggerated form of patriarchy, I figured out
quite early that I was not as valuable as my male counterpart.
Boys as young as twelve-years-old received the priesthood, an
honor that women could never hold. So, theoretically speaking,
a twelve-year-old boy who has the Aaronic Priesthood had more
power than his adult female parent figure. But what really told
me that my gender was substandard was the issue of polygamy.
I knew that I would be expected to share my husband in the
eternities with many sister wives. "Don't worry about that now,"

they would placate, "You'll have a different understanding when you're in the Celestial Kingdom."

Living under the watchful eyes and the mantel of priesthood authority confused me as to what individual rights and power I had. As a female, the confusion was intensified. We were taught that our job as women was to provide a home for our husbands and have children, many of them. A career was frowned upon. Acquiring an education was fine. You never knew if you'd be widowed. But an education was to be had in hopes that a woman would never need to use it to support herself.

As time went by, I grew increasingly agitated by male dominance and supremacy. My agitation grew to outright anger and even as I served as a counselor and eventually as President of the Primary, I had a difficult time keeping my feelings under wraps. Patronizing explanations were often the answers I received to my question about why women were not allowed to hold the priesthood. "Women are holier than men and do not need the priesthood" or "Women have access to the priesthood through their husbands" and "We believe in honoring women by putting them in a position of respect, on a pedestal."

I came to despise that pedestal. It signified to me what the balcony must have represented to African Americans for so many years. It was a station to where we were sequestered. It exemplified inequality and exclusion. It was a place to keep us quiet. I raged inside each time I was symbolically placed there knowing that once there, I could not move. I felt stuck perched upon that pedestal and I would have none of it.

During this tumultuous time, my husband and I had monthly visits from the Home Teachers (priesthood holders are assigned to several families in their ward where they are instructed to visit each month and deliver a message or see if there's anything the family needs). At the end of each session one of them would ask, "Cliff, as the head of the household would you please choose someone to say the closing prayer?" One month I interrupted, "I'm also the head of this household and I'll choose today." Although they were obviously startled, the Home Teachers acquiesced. This went on for some time where every other month, I'd take my turn, as the other head of the household, choosing someone to say the closing prayer. It was the 1980's; I was in my twenties and this *was* a big deal. The final straw came not too long afterward when I knew I could no longer stay in an organization that would not recognize me being as viable and empowered as my husband.

I began to wonder about Mormon history—the real Mormon history. I don't remember how I heard about *No Man Knows My History* by Fawn Brody, but I purchased a copy of the book and immersed myself into a version of Mormonism's past I did not know existed. The farther into the book I read, the farther out of the Church I went. Fawn Brody's paternal uncle was David O. McKay, who was the ninth president of the LDS Church serving from 1951 until his death in 1970.

No Man Knows My History, well-documented and precise, detailed Joseph Smith's life and particularly his polygamy and polyandry.[61] I was stunned with what I learned and even more astonished that I had not known about this before. Was it purposefully covered up? Did those in authority know this information, but chose not to divulge it for fear the membership might diminish? Was I intentionally being led to believe a more faithful version of history—a revisionist history?

More than the historical facts themselves, I was bothered by the idea that they were covered up or at least not openly shared by those in church leadership positions who knew full well the background of the LDS Church and its leaders. I learned that Mormonism hid, deep within its core, dank dark secrets that the hierarchy had been trying for decades to shove deeper within the recesses of forgotten history. When I or other members would bring up taboo topics, the Church leaders turned the tables on us and declared that it was us, and not the Church, who were at fault.

Blaming was a pattern—the notion that the one who questioned the Church was the guilty party. I had been misled and felt utterly betrayed. I blamed the Church for this, not so much the members, but the hierarchy who were all priesthood holders. I had been taught my entire life that these men were truthful and could be trusted. Now I learned that they were not trustworthy. If I couldn't rely on them to tell me the truth, who could I believe?

That was it; I was finished! I could not belong to a religion that had its roots deep in deceit, control, and inequity. With righteous indignation fueling me, I went to my bishop. As we sat in his office, I looked him squarely in the eyes and said, "I don't consider myself Mormon any longer and I want to have my name removed from the Church records."

The bishop, actually a friend of mine, did not see this coming and was genuinely concerned. He wanted to know how I had reached this point. Without going into the specifics, I told him I had issues with Church history and doctrine.

I don't remember what he said next, but eventually the bishop, realizing I was resolute in my decision, said I would need to go through a bishops' court to determine if excommunication was in order.

Basically, a bishops' court (ironically, also called a court of love) is a gathering of ecclesiastical leaders—all men. The guilty member goes into the room where they are asked to detail their sin(s). They are not allowed to have representation. When the brethren have finished gathering the information needed, the accused leaves the room and the priesthood authorities make a decision whether to disfellow the Church member (partial removal of activity within the Church), excommunicate them (complete removal from the Church) or let them remain a member in full standing.

Apostasy, which is considered one of the most egregious "crimes", was what I was guilty of. In all likelihood, had I allowed myself to be subjected to the court, I would have been excommunicated. They would have kicked me out of their church and I wanted it clearly understood that I chose to leave them, not the other way around. I would leave and it would be on my terms.

I told the bishop I held no stock in the so-called authority of the priesthood and would not subject myself to their procedures. I was no longer LDS in my heart and mind. I stood up, thanked the bishop for his time and shook his hand over the large wooden desk before exiting the chapel. It was the last time I would ever be in an LDS church as a member.

When I first left the Church I thought that my friends and family members, while not wanting to take the same path as I did, would, nevertheless, accept that I was on the spiritual path that was right for me. This was beyond naïve on my part, particularly since I was well aware that one of the products of Mormonism was the belief that The Church of Jesus Christ of Latter Day Saints is the only church that has the "fullness of the gospel."

I don't know that my friends and family thought I was being influenced by Satan, as some members believed, but there was a palpable disconnect. For decades I tried to bridge this gap by showing them that I really did know what I was doing, even though at times I was in a state of uncertainty and confusion.

There were moments throughout those years that I contemplated going back to the Church, not because I doubted my doubts, but because I wanted desperately to have that level of familial intimacy that I once felt. In the end I could never go through with reattaching myself to the Church. Once I crossed that line, there was no return, nor would I want there to be. It was a bridge I happily burned. To return would be the ultimate self-betrayal and that was something I simply could not live with.

My son had met and fallen in love with a remarkable young woman. She was LDS and technically so was my son who had been baptized when he was eight. I remember well the day he told me they would be married in the temple. I was kneeling on the lawn pulling weeds from around my rose bushes. I began to cry knowing that I would not be able to participate in their wedding—another shadow of Mormonism and one the membership likes to blame on the "not temple-worthy" member of the family rather than entertain the notion that this policy is yet another means of keeping members tight within the grips of the religion.

Over the next few weeks I seriously contemplated doing what I needed to in order to get a temple recommend: paying tithing, going to church, participating in a temple worthy interview with the bishop—all for the sole purpose of seeing my son get married. I had not resigned my membership yet—that came several years later (when I left the church in the 1980's, resignation was not an option).

Ultimately, I could not go through with it. The turning point for me was when I discussed this issue with a colleague at the high school where I taught English and debate. He, too, had stopped believing in the Church many years earlier. We both taught Shakespeare and he quoted the line from *Hamlet* when Polonius is giving his son, Laertes, advice, "This above all: to thine own self be true." I knew the lines that followed, "And it must follow, as the night the day; Thou canst not then be false to any man."[62] And there it was. I knew I could never betray myself and lie to another telling them I believed when I most certainly did not. In the end, I kept my dignity and I was at peace with waiting outside the temple to greet my son and his new wife.

CHAPTER 11

Annihilation

Because it is my name! Because I cannot have
another in my life! . . . How may I live without my
name? I have given you my soul; leave me my name![63]
  -John Proctor in *The Crucible* by Arthur Miller

Once I left the Church, I completed my education,
graduating with a BA in 1991. I wasn't sure what to do
with a degree in English and a communication minor. I hadn't
decided to be a teacher, so I did not go through the necessary
courses to acquire my teaching certificate. For three years, I
worked the office in my husband's plumbing business. It was an
important job for our family, but I felt something was missing.
I found that "something" in 1994 when I made the decision to
go back to the University and enter the education program for
teaching.

I discovered my bliss! I was born to teach. Motivating
myself to complete work-related tasks was always a chore, but
with teaching, I couldn't wait to delve into the task at hand. I
attained my first teaching position at Bonneville High School in
Ogden, Utah. Right away, I fit in. Teaching took a tremendous
amount of work, but it was phenomenally rewarding. Pulitzer
Prize winning author, Frank McCourt often referred to his

teaching career as his "learning career." I felt the same way about my teaching. I inevitably learned more from my students than they ever learned from me.

In 2000, I left my tenured teaching position in Ogden to move to the rural area of Marysvale, in south-central Utah. I had gotten a teaching position at a high school in Sevier School District in a neighboring county. It was my job as an instructor and a debate coach to thoroughly cover the subject matter and even more important to teach my students how to think critically. Once they mastered this, there was nothing they could not learn.

Not surprisingly, almost all of my students were LDS. Not a problem. I was always respectful of this. My issues were not with Mormons, but rather with the doctrines of Mormonism. In fact, I rather liked Mormons. The majority of the people I loved most in this world were LDS.

In my teaching, I knew the law well when it came to separation of church and state and never discussed religion only as it pertained to literature. When we read *The Merchant of Venice* I discussed some of the basic tenets of Judaism. When I taught English literature to my seniors, I covered the shift from Catholicism to Protestantism in England during King Henry VIII's reign. I did not discuss my personal religious beliefs or disbeliefs with my students. All they knew was that I probably was not Mormon because I was a regular coffee drinker.

On more than several occasions, students came into my classroom during my prep hour. Of course I asked them why they weren't in class. The answer inevitably was "It's only seminary" (in Utah, students have release time during regular school hours where they attend religious instruction—seminary—in a Church-owned facility adjacent to the campus). I would ask them, "Would your parents approve of you missing seminary?"

Their answer, "No," was followed by me saying something along the lines of, "Well, I don't either. Go back to seminary and come see me after school."

Mr. Brown, a Catholic, taught English in the classroom across the hall from me. Our rooms were at the end of a long hall. I later learned that our end of the hall was referred to as "Hell's Corner" by students. I also knew that we were well-liked and that no harm was meant by this reference—at least not by our students. I later realized that some community members took this reference seriously. Couple that with my teaching of *Macbeth*, the only play of Shakespeare's that included witches, and Arthur Miller's *The Crucible*, about the Salem Witch Trials and rumors began to stir.

In the spring of 2003, two defining events happened. First, it was my honor to be named "Teacher-Of-The-Year." I was touched beyond words. The second event unfortunately overshadowed the first. I was informed that my contract with the district would not be renewed. I wondered why not? I knew I was a skillful teacher and students loved my classes. I received very high marks on all evaluations.

My principal told me there was a misunderstanding at the district level and not to worry about it. Curiously, the only other teacher in the building who did not have their contract renewed was Mr. Brown. We were the only two regular teachers who were *not* Mormon. There was one other instructor in the special education department, who was not LDS, but she was married to a Mormon and people assumed she was too. She chose, for obvious reasons, not to correct them.

During the weeks that followed, I had several people (teachers and a parent) tell me, behind closed doors, that I was being let go because I was not LDS! At the time I wasn't so sure. In my naiveté, I did not think that the school district could be as small-minded as that. I would later realize that they were telling me the truth.

I will not belabor this sordid event as it was tedious and went on for two more years. I made the decision to file a federal lawsuit against the district suing them on grounds of religious and gender discrimination. What I wanted was to do what I loved most, teach.

During the discovery phase of litigation, the district, specifically the superintendent of Sevier School District, had altered documents that were subpoenaed by the court. By doing so, he had committed a felony. He had removed the following from the minutes of a closed-meeting at the district office. It was this meeting that the decision to terminate my employment was made.

> She also believes in witchcraft and paints her windows in her classroom black. Halloween is her favorite holiday and she doesn't hide the fact that she prefers the dark side.

The violation of tampering with subpoenaed evidence was so egregious that the Attorney General's office who was representing the district had petitioned with the court to be removed as their council. Furthermore, the judge on the case ordered the district to pay $60,000 of my legal fees.

In October of 2005, my case finally went to trial. Earlier my attorney had petitioned for a change of venue—to another state. We were denied. Nearly all the jurors were Mormon. But I knew that it did not matter what their religious beliefs were. I KNEW they would hear the evidence and do the right thing. There was no doubt in my mind whatsoever. People, I believed, were innately decent no matter what tradition they had been raised in. I spent my entire life around Mormons and knew them to be honorable people for the most part.

In the local media my trial was dubbed the witch trial. The sound bites on television enticing people to watch the 5:00 o'clock news for the story played on this theme—remember it was October. I felt it took away from the seriousness of the trial when they used this method to increase their ratings.

The superintendent and school board members had literally demonized my non-Mormon status. Apparently, I was such a threat to them that they made me out to be a witch. Had I not lived through this ordeal, I may not have believed it. How could this type of thing happen in the twenty-first century? At one point, fear that I kept bags of blood in my refrigerator came out during court testimony! A janitor actually looked into my tiny refrigerator that was tucked in a corner of the classroom and must have felt either relief or disappointment to only find diet cola and yogurt.

In the end, my trial lasted five days. Closing arguments were delivered on the morning of the sixth day. The jury deliberated for ten and one half hours. Still, I knew I had won the trial, even before I heard the verdict. Besides I wasn't asking for much, just my job back, my legal fees to be paid, and my back wages. I asked for no damages whatsoever. All I wanted was to get back to what I was doing before, teaching high school. I had been fortunate to be teaching at the local college beginning in the fall of 2003, so I was still doing what I loved, but I was working as an adjunct. The pay was low and there were no benefits.

The defense utilized several manipulative tactics throughout the trial including putting my husband's name on their list of witnesses thereby making it impossible for my main support to be in the courtroom with me. In the end, none of it mattered.

The verdict came in around 10:30 that Monday night. It was in favor of the defense. I *lost* my case! When it was announced I went into a dreamlike state. I shook the hands of the defense and with my attorney and his team by my side, left the Federal Courthouse in Salt Lake City through a basement door.

Once we got up to the sidewalk a barrage of people from the media shined lights in my face and put a microphone to my mouth to get my response. My attorney shooed them away and led me back to his office. Later my husband whisked me away to our hotel room where I spent the night in what can only be described as complete and utter misery. My gut wrenched, my weeping was torturous. Sleep would not come that night or many nights after that. I was physically ill. I was emotionally spent. My husband tried to get me to calm down, to climb into bed and get some sleep. I was curled up in a ball on the floor writhing in agony.

Morning was slow in coming. We went to a nearby Starbucks in downtown Salt Lake City where I wrote a statement for the local press. I expressed my deep disappointment in the jury and its verdict. Ultimately, the biggest losers in this whole ordeal were the students, I wrote. I walked my statement over to my attorney's office. He would make sure the two major papers, *The Salt Lake Tribune* and *The Deseret News* would get it.

Before we left Salt Lake, Cliff and I stopped at a post office where I mailed the letter detailing our formal resignation from the Mormon Church. It was addressed to the records department in the Church Office Building. I would have resigned earlier but I was advised to wait until the trial was over.

Driving onto the freeway onramp, a news report came over the radio. Rosa Parks was dead. The Civil Rights activist had died the day before at age ninety-two—the day the verdict came in. I felt a kinship with her on that day like I'd never felt before.

But I discounted my experience compared to what she had gone through. It was a long ride home and an even longer way back to sanity.

I had what used to be termed "a nervous breakdown" and I don't remember much of what happened over the following months. But I do remember wandering the yard aimlessly and breaking down in sobs randomly.

I looked for Punkin' an orange kitten I'd seen in my yard before my trial. On several occasions I sat by the creek that ran along our back yard watching the autumn leaves fall and slowly drift away in the low stream. I held Punkin' (a name I gave him because of the time of year and his color) and gently caressed his fur. When I left for a week to attend my trial I wondered what would happen to him. I assumed he returned to his mama. And now, I wanted the comfort of holding him. I had Bess, my beloved border collie that I had adopted from my father after he was killed in an auto accident in August of 2003. Bess could sense that something was wrong.

A week after the trial, two of the jurors called me to apologize. I did not accept either one of their apologies at the time. I had lost so much over this whole ordeal that their pleas for forgiveness meant nothing to me. I was absorbed into my own hell.

The greatest personal loss in all this was the loss of hope. I realized that what I once believed about the goodness of people was all a lie. Humans were born innately evil. It was as William Golding, author of *Lord of the Flies*, had said all along and I, on many occasions told my students I disagreed with him wholeheartedly. Now I realized he was right! I remembered the poignant passage that I had underlined from the last page of the book. Twelve-year-old Ralph, being chased by the other boys on the island and knowing that he was to be killed and his severed head impaled on a wooden pike, came to the beach where an adult—a naval officer stood.

> [Ralph's] tears began to flow and sobs shook him. He gave himself up to them now for the first time on the island; great shuddering spasms of grief that seemed to wrench his whole body. . . Ralph wept for the end of innocence, the darkness of man's heart . . .[64]

That was it. I wept for the end of innocence and for the darkness in the heart of humanity, even if they claimed to be of God.

I knew how that story ended—the statement in the final paragraph of the book. Off into the distance was a cruiser—a war ship. The world was no better than the murderous life the boys had created on the island. They were a microcosm of the macrocosm. And that was my reality.

CHAPTER 12

The Dark Night of the Soul

There is no coming to consciousness without pain.
People will do anything, no matter how absurd, to
avoid facing their own soul. One does not become
enlightened by imagining figures of light, but by
making the darkness conscious.

-Carl Gustav Jung

Saint John of the Cross, a sixteenth century Spanish mystic,
wrote extensively on the dark night of the soul. He viewed
these seemingly dismal periods as transformative passages that
had the capacity to move us into a deeper realm of spiritual
understanding and enlightenment. Throughout our lives we can
experience many dark nights, some more intense and longer in
duration than others. One may feel depressed, but the dark night
is not the same as a clinical depression which should be treated
by a physician and mental health professional. The dark night is
about the spirit and the stripping away of the false identity—the
counterfeit self—and stepping away from the illusions of our old
life before entering the light of Source.[65]

An analogy used to describe what it's like to navigate
through the dark night of the soul is seen in Sue Monk Kidd's
book, *When the Heart Waits.*

Imagine you're in a huge mansion on a very dark night. There are no lights in the house and you see absolutely nothing. Now imagine that someone or something has just opened a music box somewhere in the mansion just before they leave the premises. You hear the music but you're not sure where it's coming from. You plead for the opener to help you find the origin of the music, but you get no answer. You feel completely abandoned—well almost, because you can still identify the music through your sense of hearing. Following the sound may not be as effective as having sight to guide you, but it's all you have at the moment. You follow the sound even as you feel abandoned.[66] It is here, in this place of abandonment and desolation, where you can finally learn what is necessary to move toward a new understanding of reality.

The darkness that is a prerequisite for new life is too often viewed as a negative. We want enlightenment without it, but it's essential that we pass through this chasm. We will not reach Stage 5 without it because it's through this passage that we allow our old lives and our old ego mind-sets to die or be transformed. We must make room for a new awakening. It is "a necessary and universal passage in spiritual transformation."[67]

In the film, *Groundhog Day*, Phil Connors (played by Bill Murray) was a cynical man who was dissatisfied with his job and his life in general. He was a television meteorologist in Pittsburg. He and his crew were making their annual trip to cover the Groundhog Day festival. Phil, grumpy and obnoxious, was preoccupied with himself. Because of a blizzard, they were forced to stay in Punxsutawney an extra night.

Phil was stuck reliving Groundhog Day for what seemed like an eternity. He was in his own personal hell. At first he reacted with confusion followed by anger. Then he shifted into self-indulgence. After that, he became suicidal and tried to escape his circumstances, killing himself over and over only to awaken in Groundhog Day again.

There came a time, after his "dark night of the soul" phase where he realized that it was up to him to make the best of his circumstances. He signed up for piano lessons and began to think of others during the course of the day. He helped three older women change a flat tire and he caught a boy falling out of a tree. He saved a man from choking to death by performing the Heimlich maneuver. He did this day after day after day. But it was an old homeless man, shivering in the bitter cold of a Pennsylvania night that made the greatest impact on Phil. Over the course of reliving the same day, he covered the man with a blanket, took him for a hot bowl of soup, and finally, got him to the hospital when he realized the man was sick. Phil was greatly distressed when he was told by a hospital worker that the old man had died. How did this happen?

The once self-centered and non-caring Phil Connors was now living a life of what could be considered the life of a mystic. We never saw him pray nor did we see him attend church, but what we did see was Phil developing talents he already had, learning to play the piano beautifully and reciting French poetry. We saw him treating others with loving care and deep compassion. His focus turned from ego-centered to other-centered and he did this with love. This was transcendent living. He surpassed the mundane, lived through the dark night of the soul and entered the realm of the divine when he realized his life's purpose was to serve others. It was only then that he was able to leave Groundhog Day.[68]

God died for me at the end of the trial and I was thrust into my own perpetual Groundhog Day. I experienced bleak periods during the course of my life, but never had they been so unbearable. I abhorred humanity and did not want to be part of it anymore. I turned to alcohol, something I rarely did before. But now I drank to oblivion as often as I could in an attempt to escape my dreaded existence.

My pattern was to self-sabotage whenever I made any type of resolution to get my life together. I was in a place of vulnerability where I entered into the dark, dank basement of my soul to bring up the putrefying dung of my psyche. I knew I needed to face the demons that haunted me, but I did not have the courage to do it. I drank instead.

I lived in a world of chaos. When I would attempt to curb my drinking, I simply could not face what was bubbling forth so I kept going back to my escape into the abyss of the bottle. I tried to write, but confusion set in that threatened to thwart this process. 'How can I write,' I lamented, 'if I don't know what I'm doing or what's going to happen?'

The weeks rolled by and I plunged deep into the darkest of my shadow beliefs, "I Am Worthless." I could accept that I was arrogant and boastful, that I was a liar and an idiot. I could even tackle, I was a lousy wife, a disengaged daughter, a substandard mother, a flighty friend. But these shadow qualities seemed to be tiny raindrops under a low dark cloud of "I am worthless." I could rid myself of all the raindrops, but the cloud still existed. I was in a wasteland of hopelessness and the path out of this was the unthinkable, putting my soul down on paper, facing my darkest shadow, splaying my heart wide open.

I remembered reading somewhere that we tend to live out our favorite fairytale from childhood. I hadn't thought about *The Ugly Duckling* for some time, but I thought of it now. It had been my favorite tale for as far back as I remembered and as an adult I nostalgically bought a digital version for my e-reader.

Now I considered the story and how it related to my current circumstances. True, I was born into a situation where I felt strangely misaligned. I didn't quite fit in, but I wanted to. Like the ugly duckling (who, if you remember the story, was actually a swan who hatched in a nest of ducklings) I tried to adjust. I paddled my way through the Church, through my family that I wanted to please by being someone who they could approve of. Even more, I wanted to be a person they could respect and revere. Perhaps I received that, but I didn't really perceive it.

I knew that one of the products of Mormonism was the sense of moral and religious superiority, an impenetrable belief that there was only one true church on the face of the whole earth and theirs was it. Not accepting it puts one at a disadvantage, particularly living in Utah. But worse still, having it and then discarding it could put one in disfavor far worse than never having been a member. The loss of my teaching position at the high school was indicative of this.

Like the ugly duckling, I tried to fit in but my efforts failed. There was a place in my psyche that knew early on that the Church was not a match for me. So I wandered searching for my true home, my authentic identity. I felt alone swimming through unfamiliar waters wanting someone, anyone to tell me what to do next.

I had not gotten to the end of the tale in my own life. Could it be that, like the ugly duckling, I would eventually discover the truth of who I was and know it was beautiful? Was I foolish to allow myself this glimmer of hope? Wouldn't I just risk being rejected, yet again? Where to turn and what to do next was a mystery to me, so I dog-paddle in a pond seemingly heading nowhere.

A particularly ominous dark night of the soul came to a head on February 1, 2006, when I came closer to suicide than ever before. I *did not* want to be on this planet anymore! I detested the thought of sharing it with such abhorrent creatures that comprised humanity. But I also did not want to leave a suicide as my legacy to my children and grandchildren. The following day, Groundhog Day was my youngest son's birthday. I knew if I killed myself, his birthdays would be forever marred with the anniversary of my death.

I reached out to my beloved friend, Paula, who had always been by my side through the trials of life. She talked me through the worst of the pain. I hung up with her and called a professional. My work with the therapist led me to face my deepest fears.

One day I took my "I am worthless" self on a drive—alone. My husband and I had gotten into the habit of taking drives each weekend. Our favorite destination took us along a frontage road that passed the Fremont Indian State Park and Museum. We passed Native American pictographs and bone-shaped rock formations as we traveled alongside Clear Creek. Rarely did we pass other cars. Traveling this path would often thrust me into clarity where I was able to think freely, where natural creative impulses found their way to the surface. It was a safe and holy path.

On that day, I set forth the intention that before I arrived back home, I would come to some sort of resolution. I began this sojourn in sobs and verbal proclamations of, "I am worthless!" I kept reminding myself to stay in the process. I resisted the urge to turn on the radio which I knew would drive me back into my head. I needed to stay put and endure this dreadful episode. True to my intention, I made it home with a new sense of resolve.

I sat in my own silence; I gave my pain, my troubles to whatever "gods there be." I listened intently. The words, "I Am Enough," came to me. "I am enough; I am enough; I am enough." They were followed by, "You *are* enough; you *are* enough; you *are* enough." I wrote these phrases three times on an index card. At the bottom of the card I added, "And so is everybody else."

This particular dark night that lasted for months was the death of who I thought I was. My old perception of the world passed away. I no longer felt like the same person I once was. But I hadn't yet made the passage into the deeper dimension of spirit.

A profound paradigm shift was occurring and I surrendered my life to something else that I could not yet name. I still needed to spend time cocooning before I would be able to take flight, but I trusted that I would know when I was ready. I no longer felt lost, but I was living with ambiguity about my future. I felt assured that out of this place of obscurity where acceptance and surrender lived, an organic outgrowth of trust, understanding, and direction would propel me into the next phase of my life.

James Fowler said you can't get hit by the train if you're not on the track.[69] It was a rather violent way of saying that in order to move from the fourth stage of faith to the fifth, you must have a practice that gets you there, be it meditation, prayer, or some other daily devotion that, whether you believed it or not, kept you ripe for the seed of renewed life to sprout within. It was time for me to stand in the middle of the track and wait for that train.

CHAPTER 13

Daily Spiritual Practice

A ritual becomes the match that lights the kindred
celebration candle of sacred moments long ago...
tantalizing these entombed spirits to surface again.

— Wes Adamson

A regular daily practice keeps us in a frame of mind and
spirit to receive whatever it is we need to receive. There
are a number of practices that seem to open a person's heart to
receiving the desired peace and quiet assurance.

The good news was that I didn't have to clean myself up to
begin. I started with where I was, asking myself if I already
had a daily practice in place. I did. It was my daily coffee
ritual.

Recently, my husband asked me what beverage, other than
water, would I be least likely to give up. I had already stopped
drinking alcohol, so that wasn't it. I love milk, but I drank
it because it was cold and tasted good. But my coffee, two
cups each morning, served several purposes. It was warm and
pleasant tasting, especially since I had perfected the art of coffee
making. By the end of the first cup, I was already feeling awake
and alert. But most importantly, my coffee time was when I
could drop into whispered reflection.

I always drank my coffee slowly, deliberately and by the time I finished, I was ready to start the day. Coffee, and sometimes tea, was also the beverage I served when I had my friends over for a visit. Over steaming cups we delved into topics like parallel universes, ghosts, reincarnation, and psychic abilities.

The answer to my husband's question was definitely coffee. I started there. Later I would include into my daily spiritual practice guided meditation, journaling, mindfulness, and exercise, but for now, it was coffee.

Over the next few months I slowly crept out of the mire that was my life and wrote my way back to lucidity. I began journaling every morning as a practice, following the guidelines of Julia Cameron's book *The Artist's Way*.[70] Initially, my writings were a hodgepodge of emotions erratically scratched down on paper. But in time, they began to take form. I browsed back and was struck with what I was reading. I began writing other pieces, apart from my morning pages, and kept them neatly organized in a writing portfolio.

In May of 2006, an opportunity sprang into my life quite unexpectedly. I was asked to be the copy editor and a contributor for a southwest regional magazine. I was honored that someone took a chance with me. I was eager to begin and have been gratefully associated with the magazine ever since.

Another door would soon open. I made the decision to run for school board member. It was for my own local district, Piute, not Sevier County where I had previously taught. I ran a campaign and won. With these two developments along with teaching at the college, I kept busy with what I loved. My life took an encouraging turn. It seemed that events were falling into a pattern—a rhythm.

In the fall of 2006, I ran into a neighbor in the local grocery store. As we talked she mentioned a little orange kitten she found by the creek the year before, in October. It was mewing for his mama that would not come. I realized this was my little orange kitten, Punkin' who comforted me as I sat by the creek just before my trial. I cried with joy and relief, a second chance!

"What did you name him?" I asked.

"Sweet William," she answered.

The simple change of including daily spiritual practices altered my energy. I was noticeably more content with my life. I increased my practices, now spending time in hushed stillness, away from even my pre-recorded guided meditations. I began keeping a gratitude journal and wrote down five things I was grateful for every day.

I encouraged anyone I could to begin a daily practice if they didn't already have one. If they liked to pray, this was where they could start. If they didn't pray formally, then quiet moments served the same purpose. Some people practiced yoga, walking meditations, and reading inspirational books or scripture.

Setting an intention to live in the moment can be a powerful practice to begin. If it takes everything you've got to get out of bed each morning, shower, and get dressed, then turn that into a sacred daily practice. Taking time to do nothing *is* something. Once you've been working on a daily practice for a period of time, you can add another one or switch completely, if that suits you. Listen intently to your own intuition. Do what resonates with you. The purpose of a daily practice is to cultivate living our lives with awareness. From there, it's only a matter of time before the train comes by that will transport us into Stage 5.

STAGE FIVE

Conjunctive Faith

CHAPTER 14

Beyond the Ego

I never made one of my discoveries through the
process of rational thinking.

-Albert Einstein

In F. Scott Fitzgerald's *The Great Gatsby*, Nick Caraway, the
protagonist, sees a green light across the shadowy waters
of Manhasset Bay on Long Island. The light is described as
"minute and far away,"[71] and it seems almost impossible to reach.
We find out later in the novel that it's the light at the end of
Daisy Buchanan's dock. Nick, "stretched out his arms toward
the dark water in a curious way . . ."[72] The green light is symbolic
of Nick's dream of having Daisy. On a larger scale, it represents
the American dream, materialistic as it is. Its distance embodies
the seeming impossibility of acquiring the dream. And, in fact,
in the end, the dream is not realized for Nick.

I use the green light, however, as a symbol of the hope that
can help us navigate our way through the difficulties of Stage
4 as we hold fast to the green light that shines on the other side
of the murky waters.

Hope is what Stage 5 is for us while we're still in the throes
of the dark night. Focusing our vision on the green light and
standing in the track, we know we will reach that which is most

precious, the transformation that will envelop us in the light of transcendent understanding.

Fowler begins his chapter on Stage 5 with, "I have not found or fabricated a simple way to describe Conjunctive faith. . . The truth, I believe, is that Stage 5, as a style of faith-knowing, *does* exist and it *is* complex." He goes on to state that, while we know by the writings of some people that they are at this level of faith development, "its structural features have not been adequately described. . . "[73] I have to agree. They have not been adequately described because they *cannot* be described. The "they" that is being spoken of is beyond the boundaries of form, language, thought, logic, ego, and anything else that we equate with the manifest world and the conceptual human brain.

Whatever words we use to describe the indescribable are, at best, merely pointers or indicators to whatever "It" is. But before I continue describing that which cannot be described, let me complete my setup for Stage 5.

Rarely does one reach this stage, known as Conjunctive Faith, before middle-age. It seems to take years of life experiences to prepare us for growth into this realm. But once we're here, life is seen as paradoxical. Deepak Chopra describes the human soul as, "a place of ambiguity, paradox, and contradiction. Our experience is one of contrast, light and dark, up and down, sacred and profane, etc."[74]

In Stage 5 we enter the realm of the mystic. I had read the works of mystics from several traditions over the years because when I left the Church, I no longer had a pat answer to life's big questions: Does God exist? If so, who or what is it? Do I have a soul? What happens when I die? Will I continue to exist? Will the entity known as Erin and my consciousness continue on and remember? What about reincarnation? What is the purpose of life?

These are questions that most of us have, but the mystic, often through contemplative practices, seeks to get the answers. Exactly what is a mystic? I think of a mystic as a seeker of truth and understanding beyond religious and cultural norms. It is someone who experiences a transcendent reality that is beyond our concepts of time and space.

Mystics awaken to the realization that separation is an illusion and that our true nature is oneness with all that there is. It is a remembering that not only are we part of the divine, but that ultimately there is nothing else but Divine Consciousness. While mystics may have mere glimpses of this reality in the beginning, the desire of the mystic is to immerse themselves completely into this Presence.

". . . Mystics dedicate their lives to experiencing a reality that the mind cannot grasp and language cannot explain." It's a refocusing "from concern with the outer world to discovering the truth that we already are that for which we are seeking."[75]

James Fowler doesn't make the distinction that Stage 5 is the beginning of a mystical state of faith. But I do. When we enter mid-life, the questions of existence become more acute as we contemplate our own impending death.

In this fifth stage, we begin to see the limits of our logical mind. It's not that critical thinking does not carry over from Stage 4 into Stage 5; it does. "It carries forward the critical capacities and methods of the previous stage, but it no longer trusts them except as tools to avoid self-deception and to order truths encountered in other ways."[76]

A mystic realizes that there is power in logic and reasoning, but logic and reasoning can only take us so far. This is where the word Conjunctive comes in. Conjunctive, of course, means conjoined. In Stage 5 we conjoin our logic with our intuition, our minds with our hearts and our humanity with our divinity, our conscious mind with our subconscious mind. When we make logic our God, we automatically limit ourselves along spiritual lines.

For years I refused to acknowledge that there was something out there (or in here) that was as real, actually more real, than my cogent mind. In other words, it took me a very long time to realize that there's more than one way of arriving at Truth.

In our post-Newtonian world, we must recognize the impact of science and the material world. Science has perfected the art of testing hypothesis to confirm what is manifest in the world of form. When we add to the mix that Truth is multi-dimensional, then it's time for us to reevaluate our definition of reality. It's like the story of the blind men and the elephant.

There are several blind men who are asked to determine what an elephant looks like. Each one feels a different part of the elephant's body. One man touches the leg of the elephant and declares, "I know what the elephant looks like! It looks like a pillar."

The second man touches the tail of the animal. "Why this beast is like a rope," he announces.

The third man touches the elephant's trunk and states that, "Indeed, this creature is a branch."

Next comes the blind man who feels the ear of the elephant. "Hmm, I do believe this animal resembles a fan," says the man.

Finally, the last blind fellow goes up to the elephant and caresses its belly. "Ahh," he says, "this is a wall."

All the blind men are correct as they refer to their own subjective experience. But they are only partially correct. Part of the elephant *does* resemble a branch. Another section of the animal actually does seem like a wall and on it goes.

When I was a child, my mother used to raise chickens. She had an incubator and would diligently turn the gestating eggs so the light would warm all sides. My siblings and I patiently watched many chicks peck their way out of the eggshell. I don't know how long it took because time stood still for me at these magical moments. Eventually, the chick, slathered in wet, would limp out on the soft straw that rested at the bottom of the incubator. With head flopping and legs shaking, the little chick would struggle to stand and lift its head. Before we knew it, there would be a fuzzy yellow or black chick scurrying about ready to begin life. The eggshell that once housed the chick was now littered, like pieces of paper, in the incubator. It served its purpose, which was crucial at one point, but was needed no more.

Poet and philosopher, Mark Nepo once said in an interview that when the butterfly leaves the cocoon, it does not mean the cocoon is wrong. It merely means that the butterfly has outgrown it.[77] I think that everyone has a different cocoon or an eggshell, a place of fertile darkness that slowly changes us from one level of consciousness, where we are spiritually asleep, into a renewed and unique understanding of the world. In a sense, Stage 4 is our cocoon. When we've completed what we need to in order to soar, we can break through the silk surroundings of our chrysalis and emerge, metamorphosed into Stage 5 and awakened to the understanding that there is a multitude of ways that individuals comprehend existence.

When I began shifting into Stage 5, I had to be open to others' perspectives even if they were different from mine. When I could accept that each individual, no matter what tradition they belonged to, held a piece of knowledge, then I could let go of having to be right for everyone else. This was relatively easy for me to do with other traditions such as Islam, Buddhism, Christianity, and Judaism. But I struggled with offering the same allowances to Mormonism, a world view that seemed so wrong to me.

I knew Mormons who were fully aware of the historical facts of the Church but embraced the tradition anyway. They often stayed in order to be a catalyst for positive change within the organization. They did not see it as "the only true church" nor did they believe that adhering to all the principles and commandments of Mormonism were necessary for salvation or attaining the highest level of glory in the Celestial Kingdom. They didn't even necessarily believe in the Celestial Kingdom. But, like me, many of them came from a long family history of church involvement and found meaning in that tradition and a sense of belonging to something larger than they were. These Stage 5 Mormons had no problem with people leaving the faith because they understood that there were many pathways to the divine. I had much to learn from them.

Ultimately, I knew that Mormonism was not a good fit for me. And I unequivocally did not believe it was a suitable place to raise my children—something I've never wavered from. While the doctrine, principles, and culture never resonated with my personality, desires, and goals, I needed to let those who chose that path well enough alone—not for their sake, but for mine. This sounds relatively simple, but removing the obstacles, most of them of my own creation, was quite a process. After years of inner turmoil, I was finally ready for what mythologist, Joseph Campbell, referred to as "The Call to Adventure."[78] By answering this call, I was finally able to face the dragons of my own consciousness.

CHAPTER 15

Answering the Hero's Call

Go to places you have deemed off limits. This is the
time to take off the shell of your past and step into
the rich possibilities of your future.[79]

-Debbie Ford from *Spiritual Divorce*

Early in 2011, I became familiar with the concept of the
shadow through Debbie Ford. Her organization, The Ford
Institute offered life-coach training in the area of integrative and
break-through shadow work. I had considered training as a life
coach in 2006, but never made a decision on it. Now, five years
later, I found myself seriously reconsidering a shift in my career.

Joseph Campbell said that when we follow our bliss, "the
universe will open doors where there were only walls." I found
that this was more than mere optimism. The training was more
expensive than I thought my budget could withstand, but a door
opened that provided me with the necessary finances to cover the
costs. Everything seemed to fall neatly and systematically into
place. By September of 2011, I began my training at The Ford
Institute. This decision forever changed the trajectory of my path.

Years before, in the summer of 1998, I had gone to a summer
debate camp at the College of Eastern Utah in Price. I was the
new debate coach at Bonneville High School in Ogden. The year

before I had suffered a devastating illness that should have taken my life. I had pancreatitis with pseudo-cysts. Pockets of e-coli and staff infections filled my abdominal cavity.

In July of 1997, on my thirty-ninth birthday, I was admitted into the hospital for a third time within a six week period. By now, I was being fed through a Peripherally Inserted Central Catheter (PICC line) as I could not keep food down. I would continue being fed intravenously for nearly six months.

I went through a series of CAT scans and treatments where the radiologist would maneuver tubes into my abdominal area, focusing in on the pockets of infection. The tubes were sutured to my skin, just below the small of my back. I had as many as five tubes at one time going through two different ports in that area. These tubes were then connected to a type of vacuum device that gently sucked out the infection into an enclosed container. It was as horrific as it sounds.

Throughout my illness I found it difficult to sleep at night. I feared that if I fell asleep, I may not wake up and so began my years of chronic insomnia. In the morning when the sun would peak over the Wasatch Mountains, I could sleep, but there was something about the night that terrified me. I spent them wondering about death—where would I go? Would I cease to exist? I have no memory of 'me' before I was born. Would it be like that? I had no surety or peace of mind as to who I was and where I would go when I died. Eventually, I had a full recovery, but my questions still lingered. Then I found myself in Price, Utah participating in a camp for both debate students and coaches.

I had two goals for this two week experience. The first was to become well-trained on the topics for debate that season. The second one was something I kept to myself, not even sharing it with my husband. I wanted to know if anything existed beyond this life and I would do what I could to have something or someone manifest this to me.

Each night after the training, I would have my dinner and then drive into the mountains to secluded spots where I sat, literally on top of a mountain, and meditated. I did this night after night waiting for a sign. I didn't know what the sign would or should be only that I would recognize it when it revealed itself.

Nothing happened. Nothing! I left Price feeling absolutely defeated in the God area.

I had no spiritual home for many years, years that included a move to rural Utah, losing a teaching position, the death of my father, a lost lawsuit and a very dark night of the soul. And then, little-by-little, I wrote my way back to sanity and hope. But still, no "sign" was manifest in my world. That is until October of 2011.

A requirement for my training at The Ford Institute included two weekend intensive workshops in California and one weekend of the Shadow Process. In late October I flew to San Diego for the first intensive. It was there that I met my classmates in person, my instructors, and Debbie Ford.

On the first night, we were asked to set an intention for the weekend. My intention was to have some kind of confirmation that there was something out there that was greater than me. We worked hard that weekend and by Saturday night I fell into bed after a late and very intense session led by Debbie. I drifted off to sleep feeling defeated. Tomorrow I would be leaving San Diego and I had no indication of anything other than I was tired as hell.

At 5:30 the next morning, I awakened suddenly with an indelible understanding that I was much more than I appeared to be. With a sense of remembering, I realized that there was a greater reality that existed internally—within me. In fact, it was *me*. I had been looking outside myself for this Universal Energy and it resided within the entire time.

With this profound understanding, I cried tears of exhaustion, relief, and absolute joy. It was a simple event and one that would be meaningless to anyone else, but I experienced a massive shift in my heart that morning. I shared this realization with the others during our morning session. I would later understand that this defining moment was what transported me into Stage 5. It was the train that stopped to pick me up from the tracks where I stood in wait.

My life radically changed from that point on in ways I would have never imagined. I didn't fully understand what happened to me that morning in San Diego and I've come to accept that, at least for now, I don't need to understand it. That's part of the beauty of it all. Living peacefully with ambiguity is new to me, but it's a welcome addition to my life.

There is a story from the Arthurian legend that mythologist, Joseph Campbell, recounts numerous times in books and interviews. King Arthur's knights are all seated around a table, but the king will not let them eat until they've had an adventure. As luck would have it, an amazing opportunity came in the form of the Holy Grail magically appearing before them, albeit covered with a cloth. All the knights stared in amazement, but the Grail soon disappeared. King Arthur's nephew, Sir Gawain, stood up and announced, "I want to make a proposal that we should all go in search of the Grail, unveil it and behold it with our very eyes." But then "they thought it would be a disgrace to go forth in a group." So each entered the forest at a specific spot that *he* had chosen where there was no path and where it was darkest. If the knights had chosen to follow an existing path, it would have been someone else's way. Campbell stated that "maturity consists in outgrowing [childhood dependency] and becoming your own authority in your life."[80]

It now became essential for me to begin trusting myself and create a path of my own making. I was up for the journey. I answered the call to begin moving toward my own greatness and I was willing to go where it would take me and that meant confronting the shadows that resided deep within my consciousness. That October morning I began my journey into a pathless land where I would discover a unique relationship with myself, others, and the Divine.

CHAPTER 16

Me and My Shadow

Accept yourself: flaws, quirks, talents, secret
thoughts, all of it, and experience true liberation.
                                    -Amy Leigh Mercree

Carl Jung wrote comprehensively about the shadow, aspects
of ourselves we want to keep hidden or of which we're
not aware. I learned that shadow qualities existed within
the framework of the life events that made up our unique
stories. Throughout our lives, we went through a multitude
of experiences to which we attached meaning. Some of these
experiences were trivial while others greatly affected our lives.
When we were quite young, we may have attached meaning to
a particular circumstance. The meaning we assigned to it may
bear little resemblance to reality. But for us, it seemed very real.

When I was asked to write a little about myself using no
more than one or two paragraphs, my story went something
like this:

> *I was born a Mormon. Being a girl meant that I wouldn't
> have as much power and control in my life as boys do. I
> always tried to fit in but I never felt like I did. When I was
> in high school I got pregnant and had to get married. I was*

the black sheep of the family. I eventually left the Church and when I did the Mormons treated me like a second-class citizen. The Church was always more important than I was and that's why I was accused of being a witch and lost my teaching job. I just can't seem to do anything right. It seems everybody just wants me to be a follower and not think for myself.

When I looked at the components of this story, I saw a few key themes. They were:

1. I had an inferior status because of my gender.
2. People treated me unfairly because I left the Church.
3. I didn't fit in anywhere.
4. I could never do anything right.
5. There was something wrong with me (implied).

Next I wrote about the incidents in my life that would lead me to these conclusions. If I went back to when I was young, before the age of ten, I could identify specific events. The events themselves were not right or wrong. But the meaning I assigned to them altered my view of life. As a child I took a situation and with a child's mind and undeveloped reasoning skills, gave that event a specific meaning. The meaning, whether accurate or not, was what went into my psyche.

I learned that as long as I held onto my story, I could never reach my full potential. I likened my story to a large umbrella that I walked beneath. It was not raining, but I didn't know that because when I looked up, I saw only the looming umbrella. If I stepped out from under it, I'd see that the sun was shining and there was a world of possibilities. But as long as I was in my story, I limited myself. Within my story were my shadow beliefs.

Debbie Ford formulated a method to deal with the shadow qualities that I tried to keep hidden from others and sometimes even myself. The first thing I had to do was unconceal them. I did that by looking at my story and extracting specific qualities from it: I am powerless. I am inadequate. I am unworthy. I am a victim. Projection was another way to determine what my shadow qualities were.

Projection is when we instinctively and often unconsciously transfer our shadow qualities onto others. For example, one of my shadow qualities was that "I am judgmental." When I couldn't accept this quality in myself, then I saw it in others and found it distasteful.

I spent years criticizing the Church and the members for being judgmental and closed-minded. When I finally realized that I was projecting my own shadow beliefs onto them, I was shocked! At first I refused to see it. But unless I was willing to face the facts exactly as they were, I would never experience the freedom that I longed for. The irony was that each time I said, "They're so judgmental," I was making a judgmental statement. I projected onto others the qualities I had not embraced within myself. I had not embraced the judgmental aspect of myself.

One night as I was watching the news, I had another insightful experience with projection. Susan Powell, a young Utah mother, disappeared in 2009. Her husband, Josh Powell, was never arrested but popular public opinion was that he may have been responsible for her disappearance and possible murder. Susan and Josh had two young sons.

The story came to a horrific conclusion when Josh killed his two sons and then himself in early 2012. When Powell's picture flashed on the TV screen I felt disgust and hate for this man. It was one thing to kill himself, but to take the lives of those two little boys was unconscionable!

I stopped myself in mid-thought and realized I was projecting. What qualities would a person have who was capable of killing his own children before committing suicide? Controlling and selfish? Yes. Had I ever been controlling and selfish? Absolutely. How about frightened? I experience fear quite often. As much as I wanted to deny it, I had even been spiteful and vindictive at times. I certainly had many desperate moments. I had to admit that I was projecting my own unprocessed shadow qualities onto Josh Powell.

Now, there's no doubt that what Powell did was egregious by society standards. It's important that I have discernment and not excuse this type of behavior. But what distinguished this as projection were my feelings of seething hate toward him. I was emotionally plugged in. Such a reaction indicated that I share certain aspects or qualities as the one on whom I'm projecting—aspects I don't want to own. Does it mean I'm capable of murdering children? Probably not, but who's to say if I had lived through the exact circumstances as Powell had that I wouldn't react in a similar fashion?

This was a distressing thought! It turned the tables completely and I didn't like what I was seeing about myself. But then I had spent a lifetime shoving the shadows down into the darkest room of my subconscious mind. For most of my life I had been stubborn, compulsive, selfish, mean, judgmental, arrogant, and closed-minded. Had I not been harboring these shadow beliefs about myself, I would have been aware of Josh Powell's behavior and the consequences to his children and society as a whole, without the loathing that comes from unclaimed shadows. I would probably have felt sadness and grief, maybe even anger but I probably would not have felt the disgust and the suffering that comes with rage.

Healthy anger can be a tremendous force for positive change. I can have anger about child abuse and domestic violence and be motivated to begin an awareness campaign in my area or volunteer at the local women's shelter. By not embracing my shadows, however, it was difficult to make constructive changes in my life and the lives of others. I remained glued to the rage.

To move toward the highest expression of myself, I had to own all of my shadow beliefs. Resisting these beliefs had gotten me nowhere. I was in a state of willingness and, difficult as it was, I owned these qualities. More would present themselves down the road, but for now, I was facing each unconcealed shadow head-on.

There are three steps in this process: 1. Unconceal 2. Own 3. Embrace.[81] Now that I was uncovering my shadow beliefs and owning them, I needed to embrace them. It seemed like a contradiction because I had spent my entire life denying them and now I not only had to own them by saying, "I am *that*,"[82] but it was essential that I embrace these qualities as well.

When I embraced my shadow qualities, I brought them into the light where they lost the power to become pathological and destructive. By illuminating my shadow beliefs, seeing their inherent gifts and claiming them, I realized that those very qualities and my unique story provided me with the tools I needed to live a fully authentic and peace-filled life. They were essential "landmarks" on my map toward enlightenment.[83]

How was being judgmental a gift? It gave me the ability to discern. I questioned everything and searched to find the answers. In fact, being judgmental was the primary reason I chose to seek truth outside the Church. My stubbornness was a gift in that each time I hit a roadblock I found a way to circumnavigate it.

I took each unconcealed shadow belief and mined the gift that was tucked away inside. Instead of falling apart like I imagined I would, I had a new sense of gratitude for my story and the shadow beliefs I held.

How could I feel victimized when I was receiving such amazing gifts? I couldn't! I was no longer a victim of my story or the qualities that I had spent so many years avoiding. An overwhelming awareness permeated my thoughts. Could it really be this simple? Yes!

Another shadow I unconcealed, owned and embraced was, "I am stupid." Through a meditative exercise, I went back to the time when I first started believing this. It was in the second grade where I spent more time socializing than I did studying. My mother made the decision to hold me back a year. We were moving to a new town so I would begin the second go round of the second grade in a new school where no one would know me. My mother advised me not to tell any of my classmates that I had been in the second grade already. I interpreted this event to mean that I was stupid.

I fulfilled my stupidity throughout the rest of grade school, junior high, and into high school with substandard grades. I even dropped out of high school early to have a baby. I didn't get my high school diploma until I went to night school at age twenty. But once I entered college at twenty-five, I did not want anyone to know how oblivious I was so I overcompensated to hide my stupidity.

I worked hard to earn my grades, staying up late at night, oftentimes pulling all-nighters. It paid off. I remember the first time I earned a perfect 4.0. I couldn't believe it! I thought, if I can do it this semester, I can do it again. I ended up getting straight A's consistently which earned me an academic scholarship. Look at stupid me, I thought, going to college on an academic scholarship.

I played the smart student well. I sat in the front row of all my classes, never missing a single one. I took copious notes and made thoughtful comments. I asked profound questions. I even made appointments to meet with my professors to get one-on-one advice about a writing project or to discuss an insight I had on a play we were studying. Other students would come to me for help. I gladly accommodated. I became a tutor for the communications department. And I did all this believing I had pulled the wool over everyone's eyes. If they only knew how incompetent I really was. But the 4.0's and scholarships and graduating with high honors did not make me feel any smarter. It just made me think I was clever enough to fool everybody. I could not deal with this belief about myself in a healthy and productive way until I unconcealed it.

I needed to really look at what meaning I gave this situation with my mother that started the shadow belief. I realized, looking at it from an adult perspective, that my mother was not making a comment on my intelligence, nor was she trying to shame or punish me. My birthday in July made me one of the younger students in my class and she saw that was problematic for me. Since we were moving to a new location this was an ideal opportunity to help me through some of the difficulties I was experiencing in academics.

Once I processed the new meaning, I owned that I was stupid. How liberating it was to not have to pretend anymore. And the truth is I am stupid. And I'm also its polar opposite. I am very intelligent, too. It is a paradox, but it is accurate. Sometimes I act very stupidly and other times I exhibit extraordinary intelligence. I can claim them both.

Finally, I had to embrace being stupid. That meant I had to find the gift in this shadow. It was easy for me to see. Had I not had the shadow of "I am stupid" I could never have excelled in college like I did. I had a world of opportunities open up to me that I would not have had otherwise.

When I owned all my qualities, I could not be hurt by them. Understanding my shadows in this way took the sting out of derogatory comments. It was helpful to know, too, that others may be projecting their own shadow qualities onto me so their hurtful comments may have nothing whatsoever to do with me. It reminded me of a book title from Terry Cole-Whittaker, *What You Think of Me is None of My Business.*

Even today, different shadow qualities are revealed to me. One of the most difficult shadows for me to face was the shadow of persecution. It was something I had inherited from my Mormon past and it was deeply ingrained.

When someone projects onto me and I project back then I have taken ownership of that projection. When the collective shadow goes back and forth—the Mormons saying they're persecuted by others, I say I'm persecuted by the Mormons and so on, it creates an unhealthy cycle of blame that gets us nowhere.

To end this relentless cold war, I had to stop this dance of blame. I discovered that I had within my power, the ability to end it when I claimed ownership of those qualities that I attributed to others. Taking responsibility and stopping the blame game was essential if I was to continue to grow along spiritual lines and become truly liberated. But I had created a whole story around my persecution by the Church and its members.

I was playing the victim role, but there was a payoff in it. I could be the poor picked on person who gets blamed for everything and from that gain sympathy from others. So I had to ask myself, 'Erin, do you want to be at peace and free of resentment or do you want to be right?' For a very long time my answer was—"I want to be right, dammit!"

After years of righteous indignation, where I perceived others mistreating me, I had had enough! I wanted out of this vicious dead-end thinking. But it wasn't until I reached this point that I realized I had the power to change all along. It was not activated, however, until I had exhausted all other external forms of trying to alter it. It reminded me of *The Wizard of Oz* when Dorothy eventually came to realize she had the power to return to Kansas all along. But she had to figure that out for herself in order to mobilize that ability. It was only when she believed she had the power to return, that she actually was able to go home to Kansas.

It took the journey and the triumph over the trials before Dorothy recognized she had the necessary resources to overcome her major obstacle. The same was true for me. And it would do me no good to beat myself up over the years wasted in turmoil. Because the truth was, they were never wasted. Each conflict, the ones with others and the ones within my own mind, the battles that were perceived and the ones that were real, served as opportunities where I strengthened my spiritual resolve. Each one brought me a step closer to the realization that I had the power all along to return home. But exactly where was Kansas?

CHAPTER 17

Non-Attachment

Detachment means letting go and nonattachment
means simply letting be.

-Stephen Levine

I had dabbled a little in Buddhism and what I knew I liked. I
was familiar with the Four Noble Truths. They were suffering,
the cause of suffering, the end of suffering and the path that
frees us from suffering.

Other than the basic wording, the concept of suffering went
over my head. My thinking was too Western to understand fully
what suffering meant beyond the trials and tribulations that plagued
our mortal existence. Through my studies, I came to understand
that there was pain and there was suffering. Pain was inevitable—
our bodies experienced injuries, aging, and eventually would die.
We felt the pain of sadness when a loved one passed away or when
we momentarily missed a friend who had moved to another city.

While pain was unavoidable, suffering was something that
was totally within our control. We did *not* have to suffer—ever,
provided we knew how to end our suffering.[84] Aha! That was
the million dollar question, how do I end my suffering?

Once I understood that I was not my "story," I would
rephrase any negative response from "I have the worst luck

of anyone I know," to "When I'm in my story, I have the worst luck of anyone I know." Now I understood "story" to mean that any narrative I created around pain—whether emotional or physical—was my story.

The following example illustrates the process of developing a story:

I'm driving on the highway and someone cuts me off. I feel a surge of anger. This is pain. I can acknowledge it by saying or thinking, 'there is anger' and allowing it to pass through me. Or I can think or say, 'Damn Utah drivers!'

This leads to the next thought, 'Every time I come up here, it's the same thing.' I'm now beginning to pile on a story. 'Stupid people think they're the only ones who have any rights on these roads. Hell, they think they are the only ones who have any rights in this state. I live in a freakin' theocracy.' Like a dog who picks up one scent and then another and another as it weaves its way through the yard, one thought leads to the next and to the next until I've created a story that takes on a life of its own.

It was practically impossible for me to experience any empathy toward anyone else when I was in this story. And one more thing—it's a big thing. My story was merely an illusion I came to believe. And even if it did have some validity, immersing myself in it only made things worse and caused me to suffer! Ending suffering was always within my control—always! I merely stopped at the first recognition of pain and did not entertain any other thoughts that wanted to attach themselves to me.

It was the drama I created around the moments of pain that created the story. Eliminating the drama, the thoughts that follow one after another, and I eliminated the story. When I eliminated the story, I was at peace, even if I was in pain. I could experience the pain as part of mindfulness and when the next moment came, it was done.

Once I got this concept, I began the practice of catching myself when thoughts compiled one on top of another, to create a story where one did not exist—or didn't need to exist. This took some time, but I was getting the hang of it. Next came the concept of non-attachment.

The term non-attachment is not the same as detachment. Both attachment and detachment are forces—actions. Let's say I see a plate of cookies on the kitchen counter. I have a desire to eat one of those cookies so I walk over to the counter and physically pick one up from the plate. That is an action. I've attached myself to the cookie. Now, let's say I've realized it's close to dinnertime and I've changed my mind about the cookie. Now I want to detach from it so it won't spoil my dinner (by the way, the dinner part is part of the story). I walk back over to the counter, cookie in hand, and place it back on the plate. This is a force—a doing.

Non-attachment, on the other hand, is neutral. It is not a force. I see a plate of cookies and even though I may want to eat one of them, I am not attached to that desire so I do not need to take a cookie from the plate. It is a non-issue. Because I don't possess the cookie (or perhaps the wording should be because the cookie doesn't possess me), there is nothing for me to detach from—neutral.

I can desire the cookie but non-attachment dictates that I don't need to do anything about it. Furthermore, I'm not even bothered by this desire because I've not created a story around it, for example, "I'm starving! I can't possibly wait until dinner to eat. My mom never let me have cookies this time of day and I'll be damned if I'm going to let her keep controlling me."

As simplistic as this example is, I found that practicing non-attachment on the little things built my non-attachment muscle. I used this concept more and more frequently and found that there was something to it. A thought would come, I caught myself if I began creating a story with additional tag-along thoughts, stopped it, and just let things be as they were—non-attachment.

I began getting rid of things around my home that I was attached to because I had built a story around them like, "I can't get rid of this, my sister gave this to me when I had my second child" or "the person who gave this to me is dead now, so it's very valuable to me." I found it easier and easier to unclutter my life both in terms of material possessions and outdated ideas when I let go of the stories around them and practiced non-attachment. I realized that this practice could work when it came to the most consistent form of suffering I endured—my desire to have others accept me for who I was without secretly wishing I was something or someone else.

This practice of non-attachment in terms of my relationships proved to be the most effective thing I had done. I had spent so much of my life stifling my own purpose and staying in my story of wanting things to be different with those I was closest to. Time was running out and I knew I had to say goodbye to my old way of managing—actually mismanaging my desires. I had a purpose to this existence and it wasn't being fulfilled, not because of others, but because of *me!*

What I found was that by practicing non-attachment, love, empathy and compassion could flow easily through me as there were no resentments or stories obstructing them. I could love unconditionally those who I felt such angst toward. Forgiveness was now feasible where I thought it was impossible before. I felt a sense of freedom that was foreign to me. With practice, I got better at non-attachment, but I was far from perfect.

I had a friend who I'd known since my days in California over twenty years earlier. We kept in contact for years and on occasion I visited her. I remember finding out that she had invited a mutual friend of ours to go on vacation with her to Oregon. Jealousy, anger, and hurt bubbled up inside of me. It took me several days of practicing non-attachment to come to peace with my ego-based desire to have my friend like me best.

Trivial as that sounds now, it really was an issue for me at the time. But I recognized it for what it was almost immediately and began the process of non-attachment. As long as I am in this "mortal coil," I will not achieve perfection. But if I can catch myself earlier in the process, it becomes easier to remedy. Progress, is the key here, certainly not perfection.

In the final analysis, I came to understand and accept that another's processes, while different from mine, were exactly what they needed at the time. And I was where I needed to be in my own evolution of faith. I was also willing to entertain the idea that the way I *thought* other people viewed me may not be accurate at all. It could have simply been my own storyline where I presumed to know what was going on in their minds. But what I came to understand about non-attachment was that ultimately, none of that really matters anyway. Once I freed myself from the attachment to story, the suffering that I created in my life began to disappear.

CHAPTER 18

Forgiveness

To forgive is to set a prisoner free and discover that
the prisoner was you.

                                              -Lewis B. Smedes

It was a beautiful spring day. The Buddha was taking a
mindful walk through a small village when an angry young
man approached him and began hurling insults. The young
man screamed, "You are such a phony! You have no business
thinking you can teach others. You're as big an ass as everyone
else is!"

The Buddha, serenely composed, asked the young man a
question, "If you go to the market and purchase a present for
somebody and they choose *not* to take it, to whom does the gift
belong?" Somewhat puzzled at such a silly question, the young
man answered, "I bought the gift so it would belong to me."

The Buddha, being forever wise, gently smiled and said,
"You are right. And it is the same with your anger and insults. If
you become angry with me and I am not insulted, then the anger
returns to you." The Buddha continued, "Therefore, you are the
one who is miserable, not me. All you have done is hurt yourself."

And so it was that as I began to work on my shadows,
I found my hardened heart, filled with seething anger and

resentment, was hurting me, and more often than not, only me. But wasn't I justified in my anger? Hadn't I been harmed, lied to, and mistreated? Perhaps so, but there came a point when I realized my resentment paralyzed me from further progression on the spiritual path I had been forging.

I had a couple of options. The first one was to keep my anger and resentments and live in a small world of righteous indignation. The second option, which seemed like an impossible task at the time, was to forgive and loosen the cords of anger that kept me from the peace for which I longed.

But what was meant by forgiveness? When I was little, it was something that I was always seeking. It seemed I was the one doing wrong—always. It meant that I must apologize and ask others to forgive *me*. And it still meant that to me. But there was a different type of forgiveness that I would need to become friendly with and that was the kind that really had nothing to do with another person. Ultimately, it had only to do with me.

I held my deepest resentments toward the Church. It always seemed to me that with many of the people I cared most about, the Church was the most important thing in their lives. They appeared to place it above everything and everyone else. I held the Church responsible for misrepresenting itself to me and its members. I eventually saw through the deception, but so many others did not and looked at me as the duped one.

Ultimately, it was the Church and its teachings that created the type of behavior exhibited by the school district where seemingly rational people could think I was a witch, where I was such a threat to them that they chose to cut loose a dedicated teacher in order to maintain a status quo that was saturated in fear and intolerance. And what about the jury who I knew would do the right thing but in the end, would exhibit the same type of injustice as the district had?

I could not deny that I had been wronged. And I knew I could not allow myself to be used as someone's punching bag. That simply was not an option. I needed resolution and holding onto the pain was not fixing the problem.

In the film *The Power of Forgiveness*, Fred Luskin says that we can be hurt and make a decision never to allow others to do this again. I can make this decision with hate in my heart or I can do it with peace. The choice is mine and either way, I can still make certain I am safe.[85]

Once I took the other person out of the equation, it was easy to see what I must do. It was never about them anyway—not really. But was I ready to forgive? Forgiveness is an immensely personal process and I needed to be ready. Understanding the concept of projection helped me.

I realized that when others do harm to me (and I to them) they are very likely projecting onto me their own sense of inadequacy. This lessened my hurt in new situations. But it seemed that the old resentments cared little about the new awareness I was experiencing. I had to dig deep down to their roots and pry them out a little at a time. What would turn out to be my most effective tools were empathy and compassion.

Empathy requires that someone connect with something—a feeling— deep down inside themselves that relates to that deep down place of vulnerability and pain in another. That is where the connection comes, not in words, but in knowing. One does not have to have the same experience as another to empathize with them. We have the ability to listen to the other, relate what they are feeling to a similar one we've had, and connect.

I continued doing extensive shadow work and I imagined my "enemies" to be the little children they once were. I would remember that, like me, they were comprised of both ego and divinity. As with most institutions, my childhood religion was ego-based and soundly set in Stage 3. I reminded myself that another's story was just that—a story. Behind every projection was a wounded individual. Underneath the presenting ego self was an authentic self that still sought to find expression.

Once I reached the understanding that it was anger, hatred, and prejudice that harmed others and that the perpetrator was a prisoner to these pathological shadow expressions, I could finally experience compassion. I simply could not fully forgive until I had reached this place. But finally, I was there and I could see that my resentments had taken on a life of their own. I had built a whole story around them—a habitual way of thinking.

I recalled a comment made after Dr. King was assassinated. "It was hate and prejudice that had killed Martin Luther King." I had come to understand that the projection of shadows caused many to behave in unkind—even violent ways, and this included me. If I expected others to forgive me of the harm I caused them, then it would behoove me to do the same.

Although I didn't consider myself religious in the traditional sense, I understood what was meant from the line in the Lord's Prayer, "Forgive me my trespasses as I forgive those who trespass against me." I needed to forgive others if I ever expected the same in return. Finally, I felt ready to do just that.

Once I made the decision to opt out of the vicious cycle of resentment toward others, compassion replaced the hate. My memories no longer had animosity attached to them. If anything, they were neutral. The wrongdoers could still be held accountable and there were consequences to their behaviors, but I no longer had to experience resentment.

But it was and still is a daily practice for me. There are times when old conditioning starts creeping into my consciousness. Forgiveness may become second nature down the road, but for now, it's still a daily vigil for me.

I forgive, frankly, because it makes *me* happy to do so. As for the Church—an institution, I hope they are able to be honest and open with their members and grow in love. That doesn't mean I have to wait around to see if that happens. I have no desire to do that. But many of the people I love most in this world are believers and I want for them all the blessings that come from a healthy world-view filled with love, tolerance, and inclusion.

When it came to forgiving, I needed to put myself on the list. Self-forgiveness was an essential ingredient in my new life. Self-compassion came quickly when I saw myself as a young girl. How cruel I had been to myself over the years. It was time to view myself as precious and worthwhile. I began treating my body better, consuming healthy foods and beverages and exercising in fun ways on a daily basis. Adequate rest and recreation were essential. But my self-care extended to my mental and spiritual health as well. I continued with my daily spiritual practices and extended myself intellectually and professionally.

Debbie Ford was right. Forgiveness was the hallway between the past and the future. I found that the promises described in the *Big Book of Alcoholics Anonymous* were coming to fruition when I began the forgiveness process.

> We will not regret the past nor wish to shut the door on it. We will comprehend the word serenity and we will know peace. . . That feeling of uselessness and self-pity will disappear. We will lose interest in selfish things and gain interest in our fellows. Self-seeking will slip away. . . Fear of people and economic insecurity will leave us. We will intuitively know how to handle situations which used to baffle us. . .[86]

I had spent the majority of my adult years believing that I had been wasting my life. Now I realized all those years and all those events were filled with the very elixir that would later anoint me with the knowledge I needed to move forward. From those experiences, some extraordinary, most painful, I extracted the vein of gold that lay hidden within. That gold led me to my purpose, my bliss. No longer was I looking off into the distance across the murky water at my green light of hope. I had become immersed in its radiant glow.

CHAPTER 19

Religion

...what are most [people] doing? Worshipping the
teapot instead of drinking the tea!

-Wei Wu Wei

It *is* possible to seek the mystical life within a religious
tradition. In fact, if one is able to do that, it could probably
save them from a multitude of family and community
difficulties. But if one is to stay within their tradition, they
must surpass the structures set in place. They must go beyond
the boundaries of religion and move far past their comfort zone
to continue to grow.

I left the religion of my youth so many years ago and chose
not to replace it with another tradition. For me, staying was not
an option. I felt my integrity was continually being assaulted
by the inequity and absurdity I saw in that particular faith
tradition. But my perception is only one understanding.

Obviously there's a purpose for religions because they've
been around for millennia. They generally originate with an
enlightened individual, a sage who has experienced the divine in
such a profound way that they try to transmit that experience to
their followers who sense that there is something unique about
this enlightened being.

I heard once that what was so amazing about the Maharajji (Neem Karoli Baba) was not so much that when you were in his presence you felt unconditional love from him, but that when you were in his presence, you, yourself, experienced being able to love unconditionally. It's as if the Maharajji had the ability to mirror back the divine. I imagine that's what it was like for those who stood in the presence of the Buddha and Jesus.

Their followers, who were not at their level, may have tried to convey their understanding of the masters' teachings. And in order to transmit the original transcendent experiences through the generations, structures, commandments, mythology, and rituals were put into place to insure the original messages would not get lost. Unfortunately, with most organized religions, the structures themselves are what ends up being worshiped resulting in the wisdom of the original spiritual experience being minimized or completely lost.

I believe it's what Carl Jung meant when he said, "Religion is a defense against a religious experience." We may be so concerned with doing it "right" that our focus turns away completely from the transcendent experience. If this happens generation after generation, then we may not even be aware of the original teaching that was lost long before.

In the 1984 film, *The Razor's Edge*, there was a scene that illustrates the importance of realizing who or what we are worshipping. The main character, Larry Darrell, played by Bill Murray, returned from WWI to his home state of Illinois. He was disillusioned by what he experienced in the war and he returned to an America that was in the midst of the Jazz Age and the obsession with and worship of material wealth.

Leaving his fiancé in the States, Larry traveled to Paris in search for the meaning of life. Eventually he ended up in the Himalayas where the Dalai Lama instructed him to go high upon the mountain by himself where he would find a shelter. Larry climbed onto the mountain, found the spot he needed to be and sat on the ground under a wooden lean-to. He lit a small fire in front of him to keep him warm. He continued his reading from the *Upanishads*, the ancient Vedic texts from the Hindu tradition.

As he searched for enlightenment within the pages, he began to shiver with cold. He was so absorbed in his reading that he didn't realize the fire had gone out. He took out his matches and looked for something to light. The only things available to him were the pages from the book he had been reading. He ripped out a page and lit it on fire. Then he ripped out another page and placing this second burning page in the fire pit, he took the entire book, opened it up and placed it, page side down, onto the fire. He paused in thought for a moment before standing up and leaving the burning book behind.

Walking over to the edge of the mountain Larry beheld the beauty of the surrounding snow-capped peaks, hawks souring in the clear blue sky. He stopped doing and began experiencing. Larry Darrell, standing on the edge of the earth, embraced the beauty and transcendence of the present moment.[87]

In her book, *When the Heart Waits*, Sue Monk Kidd writes about the Eternal Now that we experience when we live in the present moment. Like her, I too, had an "ego-dominated need to think mostly in terms of memory and anticipation . . ." Past and future are where our stories reside. Practicing mindfulness teaches us that "time is not a straight line along which we travel, but a deep dot in which we dwell."[88] I was reminded of the dot my college professor drew on the chalk board so very long ago.

In my faith tradition, I did not see Joseph Smith as an enlightened master. And Jesus was more of a footnote to the Mormonism I knew as a child. I did not resonate with the structures, commandments, and regulations of the LDS church. But it took me working through my shadows before I could accept that staying in Mormonism *was* a viable option for others. It became increasingly necessary for me to accept that those who stay in their faith need to be there. We are all on our own unique journey. It is when we commit to our individual paths, that we can finally discover the elusive Holy Grail—our transcendent nature—for ourselves.

A truly enlightened individual will convey that what they tell you, what they "know" is not Truth but merely a pointer to It. Whereas, a religious leader who is still attached to the world of the ego, will say that they have the truth and oftentimes they'll add that their truth is the only one. Joseph Campbell said, "He who thinks he knows, doesn't know. He, who knows that he doesn't know, knows."

A mystic realizes that all they can offer are merely indicators to the Divine. Once a concept enters the brain and is conveyed through language or some other form of communication we use in the manifest world, it ceases to be that which we want to convey. It's as Lao Tzu wrote in the first chapter of the *Tao Te Ch'ing*, "The Tao that can be named is not the true Tao."

The most accurate way I've seen the transcendent described in words is through the figurative language used in mythology and poetry. Poetry and myth speak to the heart. And while they do not encompass the magnitude of the transcendent experience, they come as close as possible using language. When we view religious texts as literal histories, we lose the richness that mythology and poetic language offer us. "Listen to the presences inside poems," writes Rumi. "Let them take you where they will."

There is no such thing as "the true church." Churches do not inherently contain the ultimate Truth of the Divine, although some religions may point toward it. In order to obtain ultimate Truth, we must transcend the structures, which are culturally and historically ingrained, and embrace the inherent unity of all faiths—of all beings.

Each individual tradition or religion is like taking a different form of transportation. Let's say the destination is heaven, nirvana, enlightenment, or paradise. I may be taking a plane to get there. My neighbor is taking a boat. My sister is driving her van and my student wants to take his motorcycle. It doesn't matter what form we use to travel because ultimately we will reach our destination. It's important to note, however, that there are some forms of transportation and certain paths that may take us a little longer to get to our endpoint.

Imagine you are driving a 1995 Chevrolet van. This older model vehicle is symbolic of an outdated system of belief that is fear-based. To make matters more complicated, you've chosen to travel on highways that are congested with road construction. There may even be a detour or two along the way. You may have a flat tire due to the debris that you've traveled through. Perhaps you've mistakenly taken a wrong turn. No problem, your GPS or intuitive wisdom will pick up where you are and guide you back on the path that will take you to where you're heading. It may take you twice as long to get to your final destination, but you will eventually make it so long as you trust your internal GPS.

We all have an internal Global Positioning System. I remember years ago, a mentor of mine asked me, "Have you ever looked in the mirror and watched yourself watching yourself?" Not only had I not done that, but I'd never heard of it. I went home and did just that—watched myself watching myself. It was an interesting experiment and one I still do from time-to-time. Years later, I would read book after book where the author would speak of the observer and the observed, the seer and the seen, the subject and the object. Author, Michael Singer writes, "Come to know the one who watches, and you will come to know one of the great mysteries of creation."[89] Eckart Tolle, author of *A New Earth* may use different words, but he's basically saying the same thing. Ralph Waldo Emerson speaks of the Over-soul. ". . . often we see ourselves in masquerade . . ."[90]

Some call it intuition; some refer to it as our "Inner Wisdom," others, "Our Higher Selves." It's that place of inner awareness, within the gap that rests between thoughts that we can connect with and be peacefully led to where we must go.

A dear friend of mine was dealing with her husband's terminal cancer. She had been a faithful Catholic her entire life. How it happened, I'm not sure, but during the course of a particular conversation I asked her a question that had been running through my mind for some time. "What is the difference between emotion and intuition?"

A major tenet of the LDS faith is determining truth through feelings or what they would call, "A Burning in the Bosom," a term I found confusing because all promptings told me to leave the Church. I was told it could not have come from God. The problem was mine—not being faithful enough. I needed to pray harder and be more obedient.

I could distinguish the differences between emotion and intuition experientially, but I was struggling with verbalizing the contrasts in such a way that others could understand. My friend helped me put it into words. During this most trying experience, she spent time in contemplation, before mass, mentally opening herself up to the Divine. She began this silence with a prayer for guidance on what she should do. Any troubles she had she would put out to God. She would then ensconce herself in quietude until a sense of peace settled within her. It was the peace of understanding intuitively what must be done, if anything. When she reached that place of tranquility, she realized all would turn out as it should and she was in a state of calm assurance. It didn't mean that problems would disappear, but it meant she would be able to navigate her way through them with a calm and peaceful countenance. With that, she gave thanks and let it go. It was now in the hands of the Divine.

I don't think she realized just how much our conversation meant to me—how it helped give me perspective, but it did. The key difference between emotion and intuition was the overriding peace that was not euphoric in nature; rather it acted as a calming balm, almost like the release of a long-held breath, and an acute realization of where to go next.

In my new understanding of life and reality, I went to that place of silent mindfulness where I connected with that innate wisdom. On the Peace Pilgrim website it states, "There is a criterion by which you can judge whether the thoughts you are thinking and the things you are doing are right for you. The criterion is: Have they brought you inner peace?"[91] Trusting this intuitive voice was a new experience for me. I had been discouraged from doing my own thinking for years. Now, if that thought that says, "You can't trust yourself" comes up, I let that voice say its piece and, from the perspective of the ever-wise observer, let those words drift by.

CHAPTER 20

Evolving God---and an Afterlife

That which permeates all, which nothing
transcends and which, like the universal space
around us, fills everything completely from within
and without, that Supreme non-dual Brahman --
That Thou Art.

-Sankaracharya

While still in Stage 4, I began exploring my own definition
of the divine. The concept of the Mormon god had been
dead to me for the majority of my life. That was one form of
deity I did not want to resurrect. Friedrich Nietzsche once
declared that, "God is dead." He was commenting on the decline
of religion and an increase in atheism in the second half of
the nineteenth century. With scientific advancements including
the work of Charles Darwin, the god of religion was being
annihilated by humankind. While that may be a jolting thought
initially, it takes on a different perspective when we consider that
in the post Newtonian and Darwinian world, a fifth century
interpretation of God is archaic and does not necessarily serve
us in our spiritual evolution.

But this notion did not give me comfort in the dark of the
night, alone with my thoughts that my life would someday end.

I spent many night hours immersed in the horror of imagining that the entity I call Erin would cease to exist along with her consciousness.

Mark Twain's words reverberated through my mind, "I do not fear death. I had been dead for billions and billions of years before I was born, and had not suffered the slightest inconvenience from it." But I did suffer. I experienced tremendous angst and debilitating fear at the notion of ceasing to exist. I tried to find solace in knowing I wouldn't be alone, that every living being must inevitably experience death, but that didn't salve my fears.

I heard atheists say that they were happy just knowing that God doesn't exist. I didn't feel that way. Disbelieving in any sort of deity or an afterlife did not make me peaceful or happy. It terrified me. I tried to rationalize my fears away, 'I agree with Twain. I'm not bothered by my non-existence before I was born, why should I be bothered by it when I die?' Still, peace of mind in terms of an afterlife eluded me. I felt unsettled in this matter and needed some type of resolution.

It was certainly possible to believe in a god, but not in an afterlife. And the same can be said for believing in an afterlife, but not in a god. I would seek for years to resolve to my satisfaction the age-old questions, "Does God exist?" and "Is there conscious life after death?"

In my studies I had often read that the divine, whatever it is, does not change, but our concept of it does—it's ever evolving. Our old concepts must die to make room for our new understanding. Christian mystic Meister Eckhart, said, "The ultimate leave-taking is the leaving of God for God." If we become attached to a specific definition of God, it can hinder our being able to redefine the divine in a way that changes with our spiritual maturation. Joseph Campbell recalls, ". . . When people would go to Ramakrishna, [the nineteenth century

Indian mystic] he would ask them how they would like to talk about God, with qualities or without."[92]

Once Joseph Smith and the current LDS prophet become demythologized, then Jesus and the bible are usually next. Following that, all other religious concepts of deity crumble away. This often leads us away from any god concept. Rather, we turn our trust and faith solely to science and that which can be proven empirically. We call ourselves agnostic or atheist. We understand that the life we are currently living is all that there is. There is nothing that lives on once the physical body has died.

We view those who believe in a god as being deceived and ignorant. But we know better. We realize that we were once where they are now and thank---hmmm, goodness, that we've moved beyond that. The god of religion is dead to us. Not just dead, we realize it never existed!

I've had my own stint with atheism. But what does being an atheist mean exactly? Does it mean that one does not believe in a personal god? What about a universal energy field? Could I call that divine? What about Buddhists who don't believe in a god as described by a Catholic.

Albert Einstein, who is referred to as an atheist, had a view of God, "I believe in Spinoza's God, who reveals Himself in the lawful harmony of the world, not in a god who concerns himself with the fate and the doings of mankind..." Does that mean that Einstein's definition doesn't count? Or was his language just a matter of convenience? I think it was worded best by folk singer and activist Pete Seeger when he said,

> I feel most spiritual when I'm out in the woods . . .
> Or looking up at the stars. [I used to say] I was
> an atheist. Now I say, it's all according to your
> definition of God. According to my definition of

God, I'm not an atheist. Because I think God is
everything. Whenever I open my eyes I'm looking
at God. Whenever I'm listening to something, I'm
listening to God. [93]

We can have a god of our own understanding. Once we enter
the pathless forest in search of the Grail, we must forge our own
understanding anyway, if our lives are to be truly authentic.
Think about experiences in your life where you've had a sense of
the sacred or experienced the transcendent nature of something.
Why can't those be called God? Sitting on the coach as your
beloved dog rests his head on your leg, napping, that is the
divine. The smell of sage in the heat of the desert or the sound
of an owl at two in the morning, that is God. The bear hug from
an old classmate you haven't seen in years--God.

I allowed myself to get so caught up in semantics. Changing
my language helped me move beyond my past connotation of
God. I could call the divine by anything that resonated with
me. How about the Universe, Source, I Am, Great Spirit, Om,
the Beloved, or what if I didn't call It anything? What if I just
experienced whatever "It" is.

The moment we name God, it loses something in the
translation. Let's throw out the god of religion, unless of course,
that god works for you, then by all means, embrace it. But for
those of us who do not resonate with such a deity, let's give
ourselves permission to develop a god of our own understanding.
And as our perceptions change, so will our concept of the divine
change.

The god I conceive of today is one of transcendence. It has
no qualities that I can describe because we do not have a God
language. How can we even begin to comprehend the ineffable
nature of God? As quickly as I try to name It, It ceases to be

that. If I had to ascribe a quality to It, I think the simplest one would be Love. But even my concept of love is woefully deficient.

My understanding of deity has evolved immensely and will continue to do so as I go through the last years of my life. I can say this. I do not believe in an external, supernatural parent figure. The divine rests in me, in you, and in all that is. It is not personal in the same sense that my religion taught me. It becomes personal through me and others as I live a life of loving compassion. God for me is what Dylan Thomas said is "The force that through the green fuse drives the flower." I cannot describe it, but I can point to that force and say it is THAT.

As for an afterlife, I choose to believe. I cannot prove it empirically, nor do I have a desire to. As a product of Western ideas, I lean toward aspects of individualism. This organism I call Erin will die. Her body will be cremated and scattered into the earth and sea.

But I believe firmly that a memory indelibly imprinted in the universal fabric I call God will forever recall this lifetime experience and the relationships I've had. The man I knew as my father in this lifetime exists in a different dimensional plane. He, like me, is part of the Universal Whole. We are individual expressions of the one unified Reality.

There are times when I sense the unique energy of a person or an animal companion who has passed on. Is it wishful thinking? Perhaps. But I don't think so. It's just a different frequency that I am attuned to at that particular moment. There is much I still don't understand and that adds a dimension of wonder to my life.

Sri Raman Maharshi, while on his deathbed said, "You say I am going away. But where can I go? I am always here." This idea is much the same as how Deepak Chopra described death to Oprah Winfrey when they were in India. If the walls around us, the building and the room were to crumble to the ground or disappear, where would the space that we are occupying go? Of course the answer is nowhere. That is death. We simply are here, only the body is gone.[94]

I believe, not because I can prove it, but because I have experienced events in my life that simply cannot be explained by any other means. I also think that my understanding of God and the afterlife are far from what they actually are. I end my thoughts on this with a quote from the incomparable Walt Whitman, "To die is different from what any one supposed, and luckier."

STAGE SIX
Universalizing Faith

CHAPTER 21

A Call to Action

I came that they may have life, and have it abundantly.
-John 10:10

One evening when I was six or seven years old, I lay on my belly on the bedroom floor coloring in one of my favorite coloring books. We kept our crayons in an empty gallon ice-cream bucket. It was filled to the top with crayons, some new, but most with their papers torn halfway down and removed in order to access their rounded tops. I had dumped the entire gallon onto the floor and spread them out in order to see them more easily.

My focus was interrupted by my mother calling us to dinner. Before I came to dinner, I was instructed to clean up the crayons. I remember the futility I felt as I started to gather the crayons in a pile using my short arms and small hands. Handful by tiny handful, I picked up crayons. At this pace I knew it would take me until after dinner to complete the task.

Overwhelmed at the prospect of what seemed like such a dreadful chore, I started to cry. My dad heard my sobs and came in to see what the problem was. Seeing my frustration, my father, with both his large hands, scooped the crayons up in just a few handfuls. What seemed like an impossible task for my child-sized hands hardly was worth mentioning for an adult.

As simplistic and mundane as this story is, it's how I see this spiritual path I'm on. When I had the floundering faith of someone just starting her journey and moving forward, leaving behind all that I knew seemed overwhelming. I lacked focus and clarity. The undertaking seemed insurmountable and all I could think to do was cry. And then, teacher after teacher appeared in my life to help me conquer the unconquerable.

Stage 6 is when we've reached an apex in spiritual understanding and realize the unity of all beings. This understanding propels us to devote our lives to service. It's something we do out of an ever-expansive love that permeates all areas of our existence and bleeds into the lives of those whom we now know are infinitely connected with us, whether they realize it or not.

The rarest of all the stages, fewer than two percent of the population will ever reach Stage 6 although I believe this number is growing and will continue to grow as we evolve as a species. Universalizing Faith is reserved for the most radical.

Stage 5 individuals are keenly aware of the injustices in the world and the implications of these injustices to all beings. But the danger of Stage 5 is "paralyzing passivity and inaction".[95] They are not necessarily ready to "sacrifice the self and risk the partial justice of the present order for the sake of a more inclusive justice and the realization of love." Once a person shifts into Stage 6, however, all of that changes. The "self" ceases to be of primary importance. Rather, the Stage 6 individual "engages in spending and being spent for the transformation of present reality in the direction of a transcendent actuality."[96]

People who fall into this category are fundamentally different than the rest of the population. Self-preservation, that is part of our instinctive makeup, appears to be missing or at least greatly diminished. Their vision is enlarged to the point where there is no tribal mentality whatsoever. This includes distinctions of religion, nationality, race, gender, and even species.

Those in Stage 6 devote their lives completely to the service of others. And a distinction that many in Stage 5 do not find appealing is that Stage 6 people, or Universalizers, are willing to die for their cause. Many become martyrs and are often killed, ironically, by those whom they are trying to help.

Examples of people who fall into this category are Jesus and Martin Luther King Jr. especially toward the end of his life. Mother Teresa exposed herself daily to contagious and deadly diseases for the sole purpose of helping the "Untouchables." To the list, Fowler adds Indian leader, Gandhi; Dag Hammarskjold, Swedish-born Secretary-General of the United Nations; Dietrich Bonhoeffer, outspoken anti-Nazi dissenter who was executed for his views; Abraham Heschel, Jewish rabbi and an activist in the American Civil Rights movement; and Thomas Merton, Trappist monk, mystic, and author of several books, including *The Seven Story Mountain*.

Universalizers are "ready for fellowship with persons at any of the other stages and from any other faith tradition." We see this in the life of Jesus who associated with the Samaritans and other social and religious outcasts.

Fowler makes the distinction, however, between genuine Universalizers and other leaders who may appear to have some of the same characteristics. He gives the examples of the Reverend Jim Jones and the Ayatollah Khomeini. I would add FLDS (Fundamental Latter Day Saints is one of the largest fundamental Mormon groups in the U.S. that still practices polygamy) leader, Warren Jeffs to this list. James Fowler states, "The followers of [these] men—and those of many other persons like them—would likely hear my descriptions of Stage 6 as depictions of their revered, and feared, leaders." Fowler stresses that viewing Stage 6 qualities in this way is a misinterpretation of the Universalizer.

He goes on to say that in addition to being religious absolutists or inspiring "chauvinistic nationalism," these charismatic leaders do not meet the Stage 6 criteria of "inclusiveness of community, or radical commitment to justice and love and of selfless passion for a transformed world, a world made over not in *their* images, but in accordance with an intentionality both divine and transcendent."[97]

Noble as Universalizers may sound, they are not perfect. We are human. And as long as we are in human form, we will exhibit the flaws that come with the flesh. Gandhi, for example, strongly promoted non-violence in pursuit of social justice. But he is known to have mistreated his wife, Kasturba, and their sons. Although a valid argument could be made that when Gandhi did mistreat his family, he was not solidly planted in Stage 6. It takes time to evolve to Universalizing Faith and once there, it is difficult to maintain permanent residency. In the end, however, Gandhi, King, and others were solidly planted.

The term "relevant irrelevance" is used to describe how a Universalist views others. Mother Teresa of Calcutta, for example, was the head of a girls' boarding school. She had gone to a retreat and became distraught when she saw people left to die in the streets. "Some of these forgotten people were already having their not yet lifeless limbs gnawed by rodents." Seeing such atrocities, Mother Teresa felt compelled to redirect her life calling. She chose to devote her time in the service of the "abandoned, the forgotten, the hopeless." These were people who no one else cared for. Why feed them when they probably wouldn't survive anyway? They weren't worth the trouble. But Mother Teresa felt that these individuals—all of them— deserved to be loved and were deeply valued by the divine. She served those who others called irrelevant and by doing so, made them relevant. She identified with the most hopeless, unwanted individuals.

Martin Luther King, a well-educated man, stepped out of his comfort zone when he identified with seamstress Rosa Parks and the African American community, many of whom were domestic workers. From there his ministry changed radically and U.S. history would never be the same.[98]

Gandhi, Mother Teresa and Dr. King saw the face of the divine in those they served. They realized, on the deepest level, that we are all connected. But more than that, I believe they knew that beyond the illusion of separateness, we are all one with the great I Am.

CHAPTER 22

Evolving Consciousness

> Unity and separation are alternating experiential
> states. What we call the Final Understanding is
> the removal of that which shifts between states . . .
> there can be no union and no separation. There
> simply is Oneness.[99]
>
> -Wayne Liquorman

In his book, *Eternal Life*, John Shelby Spong discusses the evolution of humanity. He refutes the traditional Christian stance that the Bible, if taken literally, would have humankind falling away from perfection once Adam and Eve partook of the forbidden fruit. While the traditional explanation may have sufficed before Copernicus, Newton, and Darwin, in the modern world, reading the biblical account in a strictly literal sense, would be counterproductive. When scripture is viewed metaphorically, it presents us with a deeper sense of meaning.

We know, thanks to the works of Charles Darwin and others since him, that as a species, humans evolved, rather than regressed. Pre-historic humans, like the animals that inhabit the earth today, evolved to have consciousness. That means they were living entities with keen survival instincts. Conscious beings are able to experience joy, pleasure, and pain. But they do not have a concept of being born nor do they know they are going to die.

About two-hundred-thousand years ago, humans evolved into Neanderthals and then to Cro-Magnon, early modern humans. And somewhere along the line, our minds evolved to self-consciousness. Humans are the only species on the planet, of which I'm aware, that contemplate the meaning of our own existence and can anticipate our own deaths. Animals may be aware that they are in danger when confronted by an enemy, but that is the instinctual fight or flight response necessary for the survival of the species.

As modern humans, we have an innate sense of our "I-ness"— our being individual and apart from other beings. Once this self-consciousness developed we began to anticipate the purpose of life and contemplated our deaths. This awareness, that we too shall die one day, caused us to experience anxiety and fear around our existence or lack of it once we die. To alleviate this anxiety, we created belief systems—religions. And while I believe, as stated in an earlier chapter, that religions were an attempt to carry a transcendent message through the ages, Spong makes a sound argument when he states that the role of religion is to gain security—not truth.

Once the original message is lost, religious systems fulfill our need to lesson our anxiety and fear around life and inevitable death. No doubt, religion has served a vital purpose for the self-conscious human. But religion has major drawbacks.

As self-conscious beings, we created religions that externalized deity, making it separate from us. We developed creeds, commandments, and rules and required adherence to these structures to maintain a sense of calm and alleviate our fear of death. We created a system of rewards and punishments where we could have a certainty that if we but followed the rules, we would go to heaven, a human construct of a place outside ourselves. These structures kept our lives intact.

Ultimately, the structures themselves became the objects of worship. This is especially true in Mormonism where "obedience" is a recurring mantra. Religious structures, at least in the form they have traditionally held, no longer facilitate our spiritual evolution. Religion, as we have known it, must either die or radically change. It's time to put "away childish things"[100] and embrace a new level of our spiritual evolution and a radical shift in our consciousness.

As humans, we are at a point where we are able to transcend our former concepts of God and embrace a new understanding away from self-consciousness toward heightened consciousness and on to Universal consciousness where we embrace the unity of all beings, all life, all that is. It's the understanding that the divine was never outside ourselves at all, but resided internally.

With the confines of our finite minds, we cannot adequately describe this presence but we can experience this ". . . source of life that flows through all living things but comes to self-consciousness in human life alone."[101]

Within our consciousness, we always have a choice to come from a place of love or fear. When we choose love, we are choosing the divinity that is us. Energetically, love could be said to reverberate at the highest vibrational level possible. Therefore, when we say, "God is love," there is a ring of truth.

If God is love and that love is within me, it is also within everyone else. All trees, mountains, birds, and fish are from that source. Every flower, every stream, and all animals come from love. Every human being from the beginning of our evolutionary journey is made of this primordial essence. Once we accept this, our lives drastically change into the realm of the Eternal Now. We don't have to deny our humanity nor do we have to call it sinful.

By integrating our humanity with our divinity, we can experience the transcendent within the context of our current lives and through the realm of time and space. Each person we serve, each animal for whom we hold reverence, each plant we venerate reminds us that "Truly I tell you, whatever you did for one of the least of these brothers and sisters of mine, you did for me" (Matthew 25:40 NIV). I extend this idea to our ecosystem as well. There is much we can learn from the indigenous people of the world in terms of respect for our environment and the plants and animals of the planet.

John Shelby Spong's views of a radically changing human consciousness may be too extreme for some. But they make sense to me. Stage 6 Universalizers may have made up only two percent of the population, but there is a world-wide movement that is happening so quickly that it takes my breath away. More and more of us are saying "ENOUGH!" Enough violence, enough bullying, enough hating, enough crime, enough desperation, enough destruction, enough judgment, enough otherness. We are hearing instead, peace, unity, community, joy, understanding, tolerance, acceptance, inclusiveness, love.

I believe in the concept of biological evolution. This next step is essential. We must make this evolutionary jump--from war to peace, from fear to love. It is time and we *are* ready!

Chapter 23

Illumination

Now is the time to see the Sunlight dancing as One with the shadows.

- Rumi

When I was a young woman in my twenties, I attended a self-help seminar that was meant to help women feel empowered. I don't remember much from that workshop, but what I do remember was the meditation the leader guided us through. I imagined I was in the midst of a beautiful country setting.

It is mid-morning on a summer's day. The birds are chirping, the insects humming, and the flowers are glowing. The rush of water babbling over river rocks sings in my ears. I turn down a wide path lined with trees. The trail is sprinkled with dappled sunlight that peeks through the leaves.

Leisurely I stroll, taking in the energy of a perfect day. Looking ahead, I see a figure emerge—no, there are two figures. One is a child and the other seems to be an adult, but it's too far away for me to determine who they are.

My focus turns from my surroundings to the figures walking toward me. When they are closer, I see the small child is a little girl, perhaps six years old.

She's wearing a red and white gingham sundress that ties at the shoulders. It reminds me of a dress I wore when I was a child. The woman next to her is very old, yet she appears to be strong.

Without a word I come face-to-face with this little girl and the old woman. The precocious child has sunburned cheeks and a smattering of freckles on her nose. She is filled with energy and can hardly contain herself. I look into the face of the old woman. The flesh around her eyes is creased with age. But deep within the iris, there is a spark. This woman stares deeply into my eyes. She is communicating something with me. I focus harder. I see in those eyes, the wisdom of a sage. I know she has the knowledge of the earth, the sea, the sky and all that is. I want what she has.

I am puzzled. There's something vaguely familiar about her, but what is it? And then it hits me. She is an older version of me. The me I aspire to be one day. But for now, she eludes me. With this in mind, I turn my attention back to the child. Of course! The child is who I once was so many years ago.

Through my thirties, forties and into my fifties, I often met with this woman in my rumination and wondered when I would become her—if I would become her. Eventually, I would call this version of myself, Sophia Tawanda—Wise Warrior. I learned to ask her advice and listened to her messages for me. She became my connection to the divine. Over time, I knew she could be trusted. Her wisdom never failed me. But in my darkest hours, I turned from her, shamed in her presence. And the child? What was her purpose in showing up? I would eventually figure that out, but not until much later.

I had worked hard at unconcealing, owning, and embracing my dark shadows. I had forgiven those who I needed to forgive and made amends to the people I had harmed. I even practiced mindfulness and non-attachment. I thought I had made peace with my past, with Mormonism. But I was not finished. There was more I needed to do in order to transcend my former life.

In *The Crucible*, Arthur Miller's play about the Salem Witch Trials, protagonist John Proctor takes back his confession to witchcraft. He will now hang for denying the identity those in authority would have him be. His wife, Elizabeth, is summoned to see if she can persuade him to change his mind and sign the confession in order to avoid execution. In the end, she realizes he must live his life with integrity, even if it means he will die in the process. As her husband goes to the gallows, Elizabeth utters the last lines of the play, "He have his goodness now. God forbid I take it from him!"[102] John, an adulterer, a sinner, who lived in the shame of his humanity, finally forgave himself and accepted the internal illumination that was his birthright. No one could deny him that, not even his wife, not even his religion.

Like John, I had my goodness too and it was time to claim that which was my heritage. I realized that those people who have influenced me the most, whose characters I so admired, were the recipients of my Light projections.

Why was it more difficult to accept my finest qualities, than my darkest shadows? But there it was. The wisdom I longed for in Abraham Lincoln, the courage I saw in Martin Luther King, the dignity I so admired in Jacqueline Kennedy Onassis, the dedication to service I respected in Mother Teresa, those qualities are ones I had not owned, but rather attributed to others. All the goodness that lay dormant within my soul, I would need to claim. And so, with the same process I used before, I embraced my Light.

There is much talk about the death of the ego. Easter is about Christ dying to the flesh. But wholeness and the deepest of human experiences exist not in the elimination of the body, but in the integration of all that we are. The marriage of my humanity and of my divinity creates a life that is radiant. When Jesus said, "The Father and I are one," I believe he was acknowledging both his human and divine natures. The holiest experiences in life come from the entire package. How can we know love without experiencing fear? Could I fully appreciate joy without knowing unhappiness?

When I was at death's door in 1997, I had the most sublime experience of my life. I had been in the hospital for about three weeks and my spirits were at an all-time low. To help buoy my morale, my doctor promised me a thirty minute excursion outside.

It was August, early afternoon and the hospital staff set me up in a wheelchair with my medications and TPN (Total Parenteral Nutrition) securely attached. I was so excited! My husband checked to make certain all was fastened. I had thirty minutes. I couldn't wait! Cliff wheeled me to the elevator and down to the first floor. As we drew nearer to the door leading outside, I could see the traffic, the trees, the summer.

The automatic doors slid open and warm air wafted in and caressed my face. I could smell freshly cut grass and petunias. The sounds of birds and cars were symphonic. Because of the weeks I had been deprived of certain sensory stimuli, I was overwhelmed with awe, gratitude and an ecstasy that my body simply could not contain. I put my hands over my face and I wept.

Concerned, my husband asked, "Honey, are you all right?" I looked up at him and said, "I am *so* happy!" And I was. Never in my life had I felt such euphoric joy. Here I was, hooked up to all kinds of contraptions including a feeding tube. I was not expected to live through this illness and yet, in that moment, none of it mattered. For thirty minutes, I was in the most blissful state of being that would sustain me for months ahead.

As tubes were being probed through the ports in my back, my thoughts went to the garden outside the hospital and I was at peace. I could not have known such contentment without the deprivation of the earth's beauty. I needed all of my human experiences—the most depraved and painful and the most sublime and ecstatic. To be fully human is to embrace all of this not just in myself, but in everything and everyone.

Compassion is birthed from the full spectrum of the human experience. And it is in compassion for others and our service to them where the Divine becomes manifest in our daily lives. And that, I have learned, is the meaning of life!

I am no longer looking into the face of my older, wiser self. I *am* her. I *am* my child self. I *am* that *I AM!*

CHAPTER 24

Return to the Garden, A New Vision

We are stardust, billion year old carbon; We are
Golden, caught in the devil's bargain; And we've
got to get ourselves back to the Garden.

-"Woodstock" by Joni Mitchell

In Genesis, Adam and Eve are forced from the Garden of Eden after they partake of the fruit of knowledge of good and evil. The fruit represents the illusion of a dual nature—them and us, you and me, divine and human. It appears in humans as self-consciousness where we experience existential angst.

If we are to look at the natural order of things, then the next phase of evolution will take us away from self-consciousness into Universal consciousness as I discussed previously. We are already seeing signs of this happening. The saints and sages throughout recorded history have given us glimpses of the shift into Oneness.

"Woodstock" lyrics, written by Joni Mitchell, at the beginning of this chapter suggests a major shift occurring while recognizing that we are physical form made of the same stuff as stars—"billion year old carbon." But it's our "golden" quality that begs to be acknowledged. It is my contention that our Universal

Consciousness must be embraced. The Garden symbolizes this state of consciousness where we are aware of the inherent unity of all that is.

When we left the metaphorical garden of our psyches, we bought into the premise that we were separate. Now is the time we get back to an all-inclusive reality, to the realization of the Self that was never born and can never die. To reach this most inclusive and transcendent of states, we don't deny our humanity, rather we unify or integrate it with the Divine that is our very nature.

Joseph Campbell emphasized time and again that our sense of community must change from a tribal one to a single global community. And if this planet and her inhabitants are going to survive long-term, I have to agree. It's time we, as a world community, acknowledge that we are all in this together and together we form solutions to violence, hunger, and any other malady that is present in our twenty-first century world.

The power of one cannot be underestimated because the acts, thoughts and love that emanate from a single living entity vibrate the web of us all. Accumulated individual acts are what major changes are made of. Remember that the ocean consists of countless drops of water.

Our environment, our species, all living beings are in grave jeopardy at this time of humanity. Marianne Williamson compared us to the Titanic heading for the iceberg. It will take nothing less than a global effort to turn the Titanic around. Many believe we are doomed to perish. But we don't have to.

For the first time in recorded history, the average person has the ability to reach billions of people with just a click of the mouse. It's imperative that we use social media responsibly. When I taught Mass Media Communication at a local college, I emphasized its ethical use. I ended the semester with a call to my students to use it to make a difference in the world. I showed the documentary *We Are the World* to students who would not be born until a decade after the film was made.

The film was produced before we had the Internet. News flashes from the other side of the globe that showed horrific images of emaciated children with extended bellies, too weak to cry, flies feasting on their small frames gave birth to *We Are the World*. Most of us in America felt sadness, maybe even dismay as we sat on our couches waiting for our dinner to finish cooking. Then we got up, set the table, and left those dreadful images behind. But a group of celebrities put their talents to loving use when they came together and "leaving their egos at the door" worked into the night making the music video that would raise money to buy food to help feed these beloved children.[103]

My students were to use mass media to start a conversation about something they were passionate about that would contribute positively to the community—even to humanity as a whole. I was inspired by Tom Shadyach's film *I Am*[104] and wanted to be part of the solution. I was a teacher; I would start there.

Universalizing Faith has only been glimpsed by the smallest percentage of humanity. I saw the last part of the counter-culture movement whose theme was "Make love, not War." It was about upsetting the status quo and entering the Age of Aquarius. Today it includes being aware of the importance of others—making the irrelevant relevant and recognizing the need to radically care for the environment. Indigenous cultures had it right all along. Let's look to them for guidance. Then let's look within and ask ourselves what we can do to change the trajectory of the Titanic.

We can start with ourselves by dissolving our fears and increasing our love. We can stop judging others and embrace them instead. I imagine a globe with pinpoints of light from one world city to the next where more and more of us are willing to take action, to not just think it, but to live it, to become Universalizers in every sense of the word.

I imagine those pinpoints of lights being connected line by line, light by light. And with each connection is a glow that grows brighter still. Each of us has a unique contribution unlike any other. Let's recognize that and use it to uplift us all. We can start right where we are, even in our brokenness. Leonard Cohen says, "There's a crack in everything, that's how the light gets in." I have found that especially in the most difficult passages of my life, I have the brightest light.

In the dedication ceremony for the 9-11 museum, President Obama spoke of "the man in the red bandana" who went into the South Tower during 9-11, saving a multitude of people from death. He had covered his mouth and nose with a red bandana.[105] In the final moments of his life, this unknown man stepped into Stage 6, transcended the survival instinct, and gave his life for the lives of strangers. For weeks his identity was unknown. Eventually, his mother would realize that it was her twenty-four year old son, Welles Crowther.

We never know how we will respond in the end, do we? It doesn't matter where we've been or how selfish we were in the past. At any given moment, we can make the shift from self-consciousness to love.

I believe that more and more of us must defy convention and jump onto the bandwagon of Universalizing Faith. Put self-interest on a back burner, push up our sleeves and reach out to humanity. Dissolve the anger in our hearts and love the most unlovable. Treat plant and animal with humble gratitude, kindness, and love. Are these lofty goals? My answer is it doesn't matter. We must move forward. Together, we can turn the Titanic around. In fact, together, there is nothing we cannot do!

CHAPTER 25

Legacy

We shall not cease from exploration, and the end of
all our exploring will be to arrive where we started
and know the place for the first time.

-T.S. Eliot

I recently spent time with my grandchildren in Arizona. On one particular night, after tucking my eight-year-old grandson into bed, I lay down next to him for story time. He told me his dad (my son) would tell him about "An' the Gobble-uns 'at gits you ef you don't watch out!" Of course I knew the poem, "Little Orphant Annie" and began reciting it to him. "How did you know that story, Grandma?" he asked me in amazement. "Who do you think taught your dad that poem?" I asked.

"You?"

"Yes, and do you know where I learned it from?"

"Where?"

"My dad and he also taught me 'The Highwayman.'"

"Yeah, Grandma! I know that poem. 'And the highwayman came riding, riding, riding . . .'"

"That's right. And 'the moon was a ghostly galleon tossed upon cloudy seas.' Imagine that; my dad died before you were even born, but a part of him has come through to you!"

"And when I become a dad, I'll tell my kids those poems and they'll be part of your dad, too."

This conversation gave me notice to reflect on the integral beauty of family and tradition. My family, my tradition was Mormonism. My dance with the faith has been bittersweet. But as the years pass I appreciate more and more the connection to my DNA roots. I take from my pioneer heritage the courage and conviction to live a life of authenticity where the integration of my values, ideals, beliefs, and personal truth meld together to make a unified whole. No doubt, living by my convictions involved paying a price, but in the end, I have received far more than I lost.

Hope has guided me through much of my faith journey and in the end I see hope and faith as beloved constants in my life today. They are the dance partners to the uncertainties that are integral pieces to the operating functions of this thing called life. I still get scared, angry, and exasperated at times. Those expressions are part of the human experience. But I also have felt extraordinary peace and unconditional love. Those too, belong to life.

I am at that stage that even if I live until I'm quite old, my time is running out. I love the intense focus that this realization gives me. What do I want for the rest of my life? I want to love extravagantly, to infuse my body and soul with the beauty that surrounds me. I want to absorb the fullness of humanity and by doing so, delve into the sacredness of the Divine. The anger I held onto for so long has been mutated by this alchemist. I like to think that from this comes a burning beacon that illuminates the way for others on their own unmatched faith trek.

I have come to realize that my ancestors' and my journeys toward faith were more alike than I realized. I like to think that they have been beside me supporting my every step. I imagine my father, now without the heavy mantle of physical limitations saying, 'Keep going, Nanny. You're on the right track—you're on YOUR track and I support you.'

The largest living organism on the planet, Pando, happens to be located near my home. It is known by several names including "The Trembling Giant" but most of us know it as quaking aspen. Aspen trees shoot up from connected underground rhizomes. Pando is the largest aspen clone in the world and covers one hundred twenty-three acres. It is found in Fishlake National Forest where my friend has been the archeologist for decades. He tells me "that all of the trees in the clone have the exact same DNA." I love how life imitates nature. I've passed these trembling giants many times without realizing what they were. Today, I stop and notice the shivering leaves, the grand gesture of each tree and know that underneath the surface is the bond that unites them all.

END NOTES

1 Maya Angelou, "Caged Bird," *Poetry Foundation*, accessed 7 July 2013, http://www.poetryfoundation.org/poem/178948.

2 *The Book of Mormon* and *The Doctrine and Covenants*.

3 *The LDS Endowment*, accessed 9 July 2013, http://www.ldsendowment. org/terrestrial.html.

4 "Super Soul Sunday," *OWNTV*, Diana Nyad, Oct 6 and 13, 2013.

5 James Fowler, *Stages of Faith: The Psychology of Human Development and the Quest for Meaning*, (HarperCollins, New York, NY, 1981).

6 John Dehlin, *Mormon Stories Podcast*, 015-017: "Mormon Stages of Faith" with Tom Kimball and Dan Wotherspoon, Jan 2006.

7 James W. Fowler, *Emory Center for Ethics*, accessed 12 Oct 2013, http:// ethics.emory.edu/people/Founder.html.

8 Fowler, *Stages of Faith: The Psychology of Human Development and the Quest for Meaning*, 122-211.

9 Philippians 4:7 ESV.

10 *New England Primer*, http://www.sacred.texts.com/chr/nep/1777.

11 Fowler, *Stages of Faith: The Psychology of Human Development and the Quest for Meaning*, 119-121.

12 Fowler, *Stages of Faith: The Psychology of Human Development and the Quest for Meaning*, 129.

13 I will clarify the Sacred Grove in Chapter 2.

14 Fowler, *Stages of Faith: The Psychology of Human Development and the Quest for Meaning*, 122-134.

15 Orson Hyde, Member of the Quorum of the Twelve Apostles, *Journal of Discourses* 16:230-231, (Salt Lake City, October 5, 1873).

16 Joseph Smith: *History of the Church* 1:16-17.

17 Lance S. Owens, "Joseph Smith: America's Hermetic Prophet," http:// www.gnosis.org/ahp.htm.

18 Grant Palmer, *An Insider's View of Mormon Origins*, (Signature Books, SLC Utah, 2002), 2.

19 Mark Twain, *Roughing It*, Chapter 16, Transcribed by Joey Day, 1872.

20 Mormon Timeline, accessed 9 Sept 2013, http://www.pbs.org/mormons/timeline.

21 In *The Book of Mormon*, the Three Nephites are disciples of Jesus. Jesus blessed them so they would never experience death; rather they would live until Christ's second coming. Mormons believed that the Three Nephites were still living and roaming amongst us.

22 Todd Compton, *In Sacred Loneliness*, (Signature Books, Salt Lake City, 1997).

23 *Frontline: American Experience*, "The Mormons," Writ. Helen Whitney and Jane Barnes, Dir. Helen Whitney, (WGBH Educational Foundation, 2007), DVD.

24 *Frontline: American Experience*, "The Mormons."

25 Fawn Brody, *No Man Knows My History*, Random House (First Vintage Books Edition, New York, 1995), 458.

26 *Frontline: American Experience*, "The Mormons."

27 Grant Palmer, *Why William and Jane Law Left the LDS Church in 1844*, (Published in *John Whitmer Historical Association Journal* 32, no. 2 Fall/Winter 2012), 43-51, retrieved from http://mormonthink.com/grant7.htm.

28 "Warrant for the Arrest of Joseph Smith and Others for the Destruction of the *Nauvoo Expositor* (June 12, 1844), *History of the Church*, Volume VI, 453, retrieved from http://law2.umkc.edu/faculty/projects/ftrials/carthage/nauvoowarrant.htm.

29 *History of the Church*, Vol. 7, p. 100, 102 & 103.

30 *History of the Church*, Vol. 7, p. 100, 102 & 103.

31 The Mountain Meadows Massacre was a series of attacks on an Arkansas emigrant wagon train passing through Utah to California. On September 11, 1857 a group of Mormons murdered approximately 120 of the emigrants (men, women, and children) in a remote area southwest of Cedar City, Utah. Only 17 children under the age of 8 were allowed to live. Local LDS leader, John D. Lee was the only one brought to justice for the murders. Before his execution, 19 years after the fact, he wrote an account of his version of what actually happened, implicating other Mormons in the crimes.

32 John D. Lee, *Confessions of John D. Lee*, A photomechanical reprint of the original 1877 edition of *Mormonism Unveiled; Or The Life And Confessions Of The Late Mormon Bishop, John D. Lee*, (Utah Lighthouse Ministry), 153, retrieved from http://www.utlm.org/onlineresources/josephsmithsdeath.htm.

33 Fowler, *Stages of Faith: The Psychology of Human Development and the Quest for Meaning*,135-137.

34 *Doctrine and Covenants*. Section 89.

35 *Doctrine and Covenants*, 130: 22.

36 Family: A Proclamation to the World, accessed 6 June 2013, https://www.lds.org/ensign/1995/11/the-family-a-proclamation-to-the-world?lang=eng.

37 Clark Kelly Price, Retrieved from http://www.thefurtrapper.com/martin_handcart.htm.

38 *Doctrine and Covenants*, Section 132.

39 Brigham Young, *Teachings of Presidents of the Church*, 1997, page 317.

40 Fowler, *Stages of Faith: The Psychology of Human Development and the Quest for Meaning*, 161.

41 Ezra Taft Benson, *Improvement Era*, June 1945, 354, retrieved from http://www.utlm.org/onlinebooks/followingthebrethren.htm.

42 Elder Joe J. Christensen, "The Savior is Counting on You," *Ensign*, Nov 1996, 39.

43 John Shelby Spong, *Eternal Life: A New Vision, Beyond Religion, Beyond Theism, Beyond Heaven and Hell, (*HarperCollins e-books, 2009) 113.

44 *The Invisible Opportunity: Hidden Truths Revealed*, accessed 27 Oct 2013, http://salonesoterica.wordpress.com/2008/10/27/quote-of-the-day-do-not-believe-on-the-strength-of-traditions/.

45 John Steinbeck, *The Grapes of Wrath*, John Steinbeck Centennial Edition (1902-2002), (*Penguin Books* 2002), 20.

46 Plato, *The Republic*, book VII.

47 Buddhist term that refers to an attitude of openness while putting aside any personal biases.

48 *Levi Savage Jr. Journal*, Edited by Lynn M. Hilton, Ph.D., (Hilton Books. 2011), 24.

49 "Come, Come Ye Saints", Text: William Clayton, 1814-1879, retrieved from https://www.lds.org/music/library/hymns/come-come-ye-saints?lang=eng.

50 Kay Burningham, *An American Fraud: One Lawyer's Case Against Mormonism*, (Kindle Edition, 2010).

51 Ned Eddins, "Willie and Martin Handcart Companies", retrieved from http://thefurtrapper.com/martin_handcart.htm.

52 Heidi Swinton, *Sweetwater Rescue: The Willie and Martin Handcart Story*, (American Fork, Utah, Covenant Communications, Inc. 2006), 41.

53 *Levi Savage Jr. Journal*, 24.

54 Swinton, *Sweetwater Rescue: The Willie and Martin Handcart Story*, 47.

55 *Levi Savage Jr. Journal*, 66.

56 *Levi Savage Jr. Journal*, 67.

57 Swinton, *Sweetwater Rescue: The Willie and Martin Handcart Story*, 69.

58 *Levi Savage Jr. Journal*, 68.

59 *Levi Savage Jr. Journal*, 70.

60 Fowler, *Stages of Faith: The Psychology of Human Development and the Quest for Meaning*, 174-183.

61 Fawn Brody, *No Man Knows My History*, (Alfred A. Knopf, Inc. New York, 1971).

62 William Shakespeare, *Hamlet*, Act I, scene 3, lines 78-80.

63 Arthur Miller, *The Crucible*, (Penguin Books, New York, NY. 1952).

64 William Golding, *Lord of the Flies*, (The Berkley Publishing Group, New York, NY, 1954), 202.

65 John of the Cross, *Dark Night of the Soul*, (Wyatt North Publishing, LLC 2012), Kindle Edition.

66 Sue Monk-Kidd, *When the Heart Waits*, (HarperCollins, New York, NY, 2006),151.

67 Monk-Kidd, *When the Heart Waits*, 150.

68 *Groundhog Day*, Writ. Danny Rubin, Prod. Trevor Albert and Harold Ramis, Dir. Harold Ramis, (Columbia Pictures 1993), DVD.

69 Dehlin, *Mormon Stories Podcast*, 015-017, Jan 2006.

70 Julia Cameron, *The Artist's Way*, (Penguin Putnam Inc. New York, NY, 1992).

71 F. Scott Fitzgerald, *The Great Gatsby*, (Macmillan, New York, 1925), 26.

72 Fitzgerald, *The Great Gatsby*, 25.

73 Fowler, *Stages of Faith: The Psychology of Human Development and the Quest for Meaning*, 184.

74 Debbie Ford, *The Shadow Effect*, (Hay House Inc. and Debbie Ford Films Inc. 2009), DVD.

75 *With One Voice*, Writ. Matthew Flickstein, Carol Flickstein, Judith Anne Nielsen and Nathan Antila, Prod. Matthew Flickstein and Carol Flickstein, Dir. Eric Temple, (Forest Way Productions 2009), DVD.

76 Fowler, *Stages of Faith: The Psychology of Human Development and the Quest for Meaning*,188.

77 "Super Soul Sunday," *OWNTV*, Mark Nepo, Nov 10 and 17, 2013.

78 Joseph Campbell, *The Hero With a Thousand Faces*, (New World Library, Novato, CA. 2008), 41-48.

[79] Debbie Ford, *Spiritual Divorce*, (Harper One, New York, NY, 2001), 203.

[80] *An Open Life: Joseph Campbell in Conversation with Michael Toms*, Selected and Edited by John M. Maher and Dennie Briggs, (Larson Publications, New York NY. 1989), 73.

[81] Debbie Ford, *The Dark Side of the Light Chasers*, (Riverhead Books, New York, NY, 1998).

[82] Ford, *The Dark Side of the Light Chasers*, 72-89.

[83] Ford, *The Dark Side of the Light Chasers*, 92-109.

[84] Wayne Liquorman, *Never Mind: A Journey into Non-duality*, (Advaita Press, Redondo Beach, CA, 2004).

[85] *The Power of Forgiveness*, Dir. Martin Doblmeier, (First Run Features 2008), DVD.

[86] *Alcoholics Anonymous*, (Alcoholics Anonymous World Services, Inc. Third Edition, 1976), 83-84.

[87] *The Razor's Edge*, Screenplay (adapted from *The Razor's Edge* by W. Somerset Maugham) writ. John Byrum and Bill Murray, Prod. Robert P. Marcucci and Harry Benn, Dir. John Byrum, (Columbia pictures 1984), DVD.

[88] Monk-Kidd, *When the Heart Waits*, 193.

[89] Michael A. Singer, *The Untethered Soul: The Journey Beyond Yourself*, (New Harbinger Publications, Inc. Oakland, CA, 2007), 14.

[90] Ralph Waldo Emerson, *The Essays of Ralph Waldo Emerson*, "The Over-Soul", E-edition, Location 2029.

[91] http://thinkexist.com/quotes/peace_pilgrim/.

[92] *An Open Life: Joseph Campbell in Conversation with Michael Toms*, 55.

[93] Pete Seeger, *Think Atheist*, accessed 4 Feb. 2014, http://www.thinkatheist.com/forum/topics/pete-seeger.

[94] "Super Soul Sunday," *OWNTV*, Oprah and Deepak in India, Apr 29, 2012.

[95] Fowler, *Stages of Faith: The Psychology of Human Development and the Quest for Meaning*, 198.

[96] Fowler, *Stages of Faith: The Psychology of Human Development and the Quest for Meaning*, 200.

[97] Fowler, *Stages of Faith: The Psychology of Human Development and the Quest for Meaning*, 201.

[98] Fowler, *Stages of Faith: The Psychology of Human Development and the Quest for Meaning*, 203.

[99] Wayne Liquorman, *Never Mind*, (Advaita Press, Redondo Beach, CA, 2004), 21-22.

[100] John Shelby Spong, *Eternal Life: A New Vision, Beyond Religion, Beyond Theism, Beyond Heaven and Hell*, (HarperCollins e-books, 2009), 119.

[101] Spong, *Eternal Life: A New Vision, Beyond Religion, Beyond Theism, Beyond Heaven and Hell*, 160.

[102] Arthur Miller, *The Crucible*, (Penguin Books, New York, NY, 1952), Act IV, 134.

[103] *We Are the World: The Story Behind the Song*, 20th Anniversary Special Edition, Writ. Michael Jackson and Lionel Richie, Conducted and Prod. by Quincy Jones, (Image Entertainment, Hollywood, CA, Paul Brownstein Productions, 1985) United Support of Artists for Africa, 2004 USA for Africa, DVD.

[104] *I Am*, Written and Dir. Tom Shadyac, Prod. Dagan Handy, (Flying Eye Productions, Shady Acres Film 2011), DVD.

[105] ABC News, "President Obama recounts 9/11 Heroism of 'Man In the Red Bandana,' 15 May 2014, retrieved from http://abcnews.go.com/blogs/politics/2014/05/president-obama-recalls-heroism-of-man-in-the-red-bandana-at-911-memorial/.